Foreword by **Anthony "Chusy"** ~~Haney-Jardine~~
Sundance Award-Winning Wr~~iter and Director~~

her blow-by-blow account of raising a child wi~~th~~
~~and~~ its ensuing, enveloping guilt with heart-wren~~ch~~ "

USA BEST BOOK
AWARDS
FINALIST
USABookNews.com

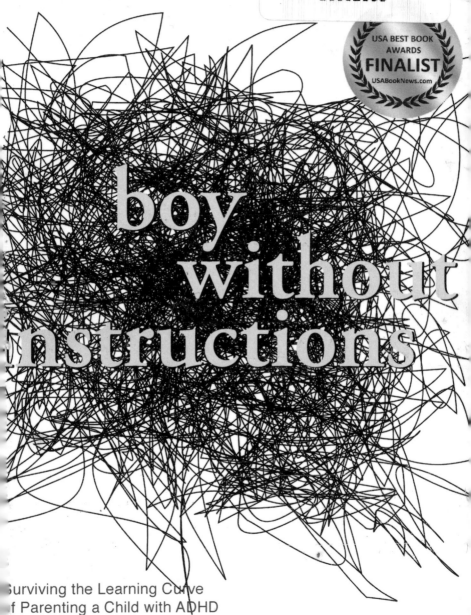

boy
without
instructions

Surviving the Learning Curve
of Parenting a Child with ADHD

PENNY WILLIAMS

Praise for Boy Without Instructions

Foreword by Anthony "Chusy" Haney-Jardine, Sundance Award-Winning Writer and Director, plan A Films

"In her blow-by-blow account of raising a child with ADHD, Penny Williams confronts stigma and its ensuing, enveloping guilt with heart-wrenching anecdotes and brutal honesty."

Mantu Joshi, M.Div; Author of *The Resilient Parent: Everyday Wisdom for Life with Your Exceptional Child*

"If you have a child with ADHD living on the liminal line of accepted disability (at least according to educational legal standards) you will find yourself taking notes on the journey of Ricochet, a colorful boy struggling to scribble literally and figuratively between the lines of a mainstream expectation of childhood. Williams lets you watch over her shoulder, as she makes decisions that will affect the whole of her son's life and that of his family. What you learn could enliven your courage to firmly draw your own lines as you step up in advocacy for the needs of your child living with ADHD."

Patricia O. Quinn, M.D.; Developmental Pediatrician; Author of over 20 books on ADHD, including *Putting on the Brakes: A Young People's Guide to Understanding ADHD*

"When your child is diagnosed with a disability, it's difficult to know where to turn. Penny Williams has made the path easier for you as she takes you along on her journey of discovery and acceptance. *Boy Without Instructions* is a compassionate story that will captivate your heart, while providing a wealth of information for your brain. A must read for all mothers (and fathers, too) of children with ADHD."

This book is remarkable. *Boy Without Instructions* reads like a novel, gripping the reader's interest with every page, every word. But Penny Williams isn't making up stories; she's living them. She paints a painfully realistic picture of life as a mom who has a gifted child with ADHD and other special needs. You laugh, you cry and you shake your head in disbelief at the struggles she has faced every single day caring for her special boy. Your heart will ache as you join her at school meetings. You hold your breath as you pray for a calm day in the Williams' household. You will be simply amazed at the tenaciousness of a mom searching everywhere to find help for her son.

This is a story of a mother's deep love for her (very challenging) son who came into the world without instructions and how she learned step-by-step how to raise him. Her courage, strength, and compassion shine through — she never gives up and openly shares the lessons she's learned and continues to learn.

I would recommend this book to anyone who is interested or needs to see what family life really is like when ADHD and special needs are in the mix. Well done!

For an anxious, type-A momma who doesn't like roller-coasters, ADHD can be the wildest ride — and so it has been for Penny Williams. We experience every emotion known to parenthood as she takes us with her on her adventure, from joy to agony and everything in between. As a fellow traveler, it's remarkable how familiar her story feels. *Boy Without Instructions* is a gift to ADHD parents – informative, yet cautionary, for parents dealing with a new diagnosis, and validating, yet bittersweet, for those of us who've shared the ride.

Susan Caughman, Editor-in-Chief, *ADDitude Magazine*

Can it really be so hard to raise a child with ADHD? Penny Williams' book vividly brings to life the daily difficulties (and successes) of getting correct diagnoses, medication trial and error, enlisting help at school, maintaining a calm family home, and more. Read this well-written, empathetic book right away, feel less alone, and take away not only moral support but also valuable strategies for helping your child, yourself, and your family.

Boy Without Instructions

Surviving the Learning Curve of
Parenting a Child with ADHD

By Penny Williams

Grace-Everett Press

Published in the United States by Grace-Everett Press

www.Grace-EverettPress.com

ISBN 978-0-9916178-0-7

Printed in the United States of America

First Edition

For my favorite boy in the whole wide world,
your momma couldn't love you more.

Foreword

Malcriado.

This is a word I heard a lot growing up in Venezuela. Malcriado. Malcriado. ¡Tú sí eres malcriado! You are a malcriado!

It was (and still is) a word used in that culture to describe fidgety kids — kids that couldn't help themselves, kids that would apparently follow their caprice and go from one thing to another, to and fro, like wandering hummingbirds, often uninterested in the consequences. It was a word I heard a lot — a word that was often directed at me.

The literal (and apropos) translation from Spanish to English of the word malcriado, is "badly raised." Merriam Webster also adds: "rude, pampered, boorish, naughty, bad-mannered, and ill bred."

What parent of a child with ADHD hasn't felt that sort of stigma from classmates, teachers, administrators, physicians, co-workers, family, and friends? That if only little Charlie would stop being such a spoiled brat and get with the program, he would finally "get it" and fit in? If only Charlie's mom and dad would teach him consequences, he wouldn't get his way and interrupt class and ruin it for others. If only Charlie's parents had raised him right. If only Charlie wasn't a malcriado — a poorly-raised pain in the ass!

And what parent of a child with ADHD hasn't felt the ensuing compunction that comes from these accusations? What parent of a child with ADHD hasn't suffered the public embarrassment of Charlie trying to fit in? What parent of a child with ADHD hasn't felt inadequate in their quest to help their Charlie?

And what about the Charlie in our lives? *What about Charlie?*

In her blow-by-blow, warts-and-all account of raising a child with ADHD, Penny Williams confronts this stigma and its ensuing, enveloping guilt with heart-wrenching anecdotes and brutal honesty. Chapter after chapter, she relates her relentless pursuit of trying to get her son to be as neurotypical as his classmates and friends — from the heart-breaking diagnosis, to the search for the right medication cocktail, the right school, the right dispensations, the right activity, the right teacher, the right physician, the right alternative treatment, and until the near dissolution of her family.

She does this with humor and grace (two coping strategies she suggests are paramount for survival), and with an unadorned honesty that often brings tears of self-recognition. In doing so, her story becomes ours — the story of parents who deal day-to-day with these challenges.

Through it all, Penny finds epiphanies and bespeaks strategies that lead her to a self-realization all parents should relate to and embrace:

Tú no eres malcriado.

Y yo no te malcríe.

Tú eres especial y juntos combinaremos estrategias para tener éxito en esta vida.

Translation? Penny will provide it to you in this wonderful book.

Anthony "Chusy" Haney-Jardine
Adult with ADD & Father of a Child with ADD
Sundance Award-Winning Writer and Director

*Chusy's latest documentary, GIGANTE, tells the story of
Andrés Torres, the once centerfielder
for the San Francisco Giants, who suffers from acute
ADHD. See Chusy's work at www.planafilms.com.*

Intro: These Days

Life is a sequence of days. Quite simply, the sum of each of our days tells our unique story. I hope mine is a story of human impact, joy, and triumph. I dream that it will be a life to celebrate long after it ends.

We are taught early to take life one day at a time. Set long-term goals, but focus on this one day. Focus on what I have right now, and what I can do this day to mold future days into the life I envision. Each day matters and must be savored, for I never know if it was my best, or could be my last.

Approaching life from this perspective calms my anxiety. It forces me to slow down and focus only on what I can affect today. I learned this new outlook over time as I parented a child with an alphabet soup of disabilities — ADHD, SPD, EFD, APD, Dysgraphia, Written Expression Disorder, and a gifted intelligence. This one-day-at-a-time perspective reminds me that I cannot establish a positive course for my son's life all at once, no matter how much I want to. The sum of those individual days will mold a successful future for him. It's easy for me to acknowledge that it's a marathon now, but it wasn't always that easy to see.

My motherly instinct is to be a fixer — patch up the boo-boo after he falls off his bicycle, or repair his toy when the wheel pops off. But some things simply can't be "fixed." Part of my journey to successful parenting was recognizing and accepting that my son's disabilities couldn't be "fixed."

It took a couple of years from his original diagnosis of ADHD, but I came to realize that the goal for my son is a life plan of sorts, not a "fix." My son's story would be defined in the consolidation of hard work and great introspection about the true importance of each little thing along the way. Rather than working toward a "fix," we were working to construct a successful way of life — a tailored plan for this precious little boy's future.

Starting out, diagnosis in hand and heavy on my heart, I didn't have a recipe for Ricochet's eventual success. I had anything but, in fact. All I could offer was immense love and a driving eagerness to understand my child and reduce the enormous hurdles caused by his disabilities. The compulsion to make my son's life as sweet as possible helps me create his unique formula for success one day at a time.

The road has been bumpy at times, complicated by peaks and valleys and unexpected turns. It was the severity of those twists and turns that lead to eventual (mostly) successful parenting and an abundance of joy. This is our unique story of a resolute momma, her truly special boy, and ADHD's impact on our entire family.

All names in this book have been changed for privacy, except mine. I guess I'm out and will claim full responsibility.

The Cast of Characters

To fully understand our story, you must first know each character in our family. Who we are molds our story.

The ADHD Momma

I am Penny, also known as the ADHD Momma. When I first started writing about ADHD (at adhdmomma. com), it was under that pen name, and over time, I became known as the ADHD Momma in the online ADHD community. I'm not *the* expert on ADHD or *the* best momma around — I'm not really *the* anything — but the name stuck.

To say I wear many hats would be a profound understatement. I'm sure you can relate. I feel as though my only recognizable role is "Mom" most days, but I am also a real estate broker, real estate transaction coordinator, freelance writer, social media consultant, blogger, and event co-coordinator. Oh, and an author, too. These are just my "real" jobs — the list does not include all the roles I

> **TYPE A PERSONALITY**
> Type A individuals tend to be very self-critical. Inter-related with this is the presence of a significant life imbalance. This is characterized by a high work involvement. Type A individuals are easily "wound up" and tend to overreact.
>
> Type A personalities experience a constant sense of urgency: they seem to be in a constant struggle against the clock. Often, they quickly become impatient with delays and unproductive time, schedule commitments too tightly, and try to do more than one thing at a time, such as reading while eating or watching television.[1]

perform and hats I must wear under the guise of "Mom." That list would be much too long to include on this page.

I am an über-organized planner. I need to know what is happening today, tomorrow, the day after that, and the day after that. In that regard, my son Ricochet and I are very similar…but I'll get to that a little later.

I'm definitely a Type A personality, minus the hostility, but in a very shy and anxiety-ridden shell. I am afraid to talk to people I don't know. I would be physically sick if you made me speak in front of more than three people at a time. I am scared of all the other drivers on the road. I am afraid people think I'm too fat, or too ugly, or too uncultured, or not a part of their group in some way. Basically, I live my life feeling afraid. It sucks, but I manage. It's in my genes.

But I am not afraid when it comes to fighting for my son's special needs.

This is my story of doing just that.

Mr. T

My husband and baby daddy is Mr. T. I came to call him that when sharing our stories only because T is one of his initials. But the correlation to Mr. T on the 1980s television show *The A-Team* rings true to my Mr. T in certain regards as well. No, he's not a giant, overly-muscular dude with a Mohawk and gold dripping from his neck. Far from it — he's a skinny white dude with perpetual bed head and considerable disdain for men wearing jewelry. But I think my Mr. T would agree, he can relate to a couple of the famous Mr. T's favorite phrases: "When I was growing up, my family was so poor we couldn't afford to pay attention." My Mr. T lived in a home with an outhouse until he was seven, which was during the 1970s, not the 1870s. Or, "As a kid, I got three meals a day. Oatmeal, miss-a-meal, and no meal." My Mr. T refuses to eat oatmeal as an adult after being subjected to so much of it as a child.

My Mr. T and I could not be more opposite. I'm algebra, he's geometry. I create with words, he creates with his hands. I listen to music, he produces it. I worry, he goes with the flow.

If you ask me, Ricochet inherited ADHD from his daddy. (ADHD is hereditary.) Mr. T can't sit still. When he talks on the phone, he paces the floor in repetitious motion. He only pays attention to a task as long as it is rewarding to him — no longer. He doesn't have a calendar, and just started keeping a to-do list after the age of forty. Whatever, whenever is just fine with Mr. T usually.

Make no mistake though, he is as smart as a whip. His head and his whole body — clear down to his little piggy toe — are filled with useless facts. He's no Rain Man, but given the right categories — music, sports, history — he could sweep *Jeopardy*, and we'd have some money for a rainy day. He is book-smart for sure.

And he's also creative. He is a talented woodworker and a once almost-but-not-quite-signed musician. He can replicate anything he hears on the radio immediately on the drums, and within a few tries on a guitar. His innate musical gifts blow my mind, yet he doesn't know a life any different.

Mr. T is easily frustrated and quick to want to give up when the going gets tough. If possible, he will walk away rather than argue. He puts the flight in fight-or-flight.

Have you ever seen rams locking horns? That's Ricochet and Mr. T. They are a lot alike, which can make life tougher sometimes. Ricochet is his daddy's Mini-Me.

However, Mr. T loves our son with all his heart, and that's what really matters.

Warrior Girl

Warrior Girl is my firstborn, my eldest, my girl — my beautiful girl. She is a teen now, and in high school, but she was just nine years old when the journey with ADHD began for our family. She would tell you ADHD's presence ruined her life. I agree that she'll never be the same because of her brother's ADHD, but I do not agree that her life is somehow "ruined." I realize it feels that way to her right now, but she'll find the gifts in having a brother with special needs someday.

If I got a nickel for every time I heard her say, "You only care about Ricochet," or, "He gets *every*thing," holy cow, I'd be so rich. And let me tell you, it's hard to get rich with nickels.

It's tough for this momma to hear those things. I love Warrior Girl so much, and I only want the best for her, the same as her brother. Her brother requires a lot more time and attention to guide him to his best self than Warrior Girl does. That's just a fact, not me choosing to do more for her brother than her.

Warrior Girl loves softball, chocolate, and coffee. (She is more like her momma than she knows.) She is a talented illustrator of all things Manga, and also a voracious reader. She is doggedly confident she will be a video game concept artist when she grows up, although she doesn't like the thought of grown-up responsibilities at all just yet. She is most determined, though, these days, to do the exact opposite of what I advise — whatever it is. {*Sigh.*} I know it's a teen thing and she'll grow out of it. I hope I can survive until then.

I don't deny that having a sibling with ADHD negatively impacts Warrior Girl. It shapes her friendships, her everyday interactions with others, and, most vividly, her psyche. Ricochet's ADHD behaviors make Warrior Girl's own personal demon — anxiety — bubble to the top and fester.

My heart hurts just thinking about the effect ADHD has had on her life, too.

Ricochet

Ah, Ricochet, without whom this book would not exist. My baby boy. The sweet spirit who soothes my soul. This little boy, now eleven years old, is so kind, smart, and funny. All he wants is for everyone else to be happy.

Ricochet is skilled at math and science, and loves both (although he won't admit to loving math, because he hates doing math worksheets). He is inquisitive and has a strong desire to understand how things work. An interactive environment is best for Ricochet; he learns best through doing. He is a lover of knowledge, just like his daddy.

And yet, he has so many obstacles to learning. Considering ADHD, Sensory Processing Disorder (SPD), Dysgraphia, Written Expression Disorder, and significant executive functioning delays, it's a wonder he ever gets through a school day in one piece. Learning is hard for this gifted boy — a true irony.

Ricochet needs to know what is coming in the next five minutes, the next hour, later today, tomorrow, the next day, and the day after that. He craves clearly defined expectations and a consistent schedule. He *needs* them. Without that external structure, the chaos in his mind and senses is simply too overwhelming. Without structure, not-so-pretty things happen.

He is also a ball of pure energy. That palpable fact is how he earned the nickname Ricochet. He played recreation league soccer when he was five years old. His coach approached Mr. T and me on the very first day of practice, within the first thirty minutes.

"Your son is like a pinball. Ping! Ping! Ping!" he said, gesturing back and forth quickly with his hand. "I'm going to call him Ricochet."

I recalled that conversation a year later when my son was diagnosed with ADHD. That soccer coach recognized something in Ricochet that his parents weren't ready to see.

Ricochet was diagnosed with ADHD at age six, just a few months into first grade. An additional diagnosis of SPD followed shortly after. Then, one at a time, his learning disabilities were unveiled. This boy has the deck stacked against him, yet he's the kindest, most empathetic eleven-year-old boy you'll ever meet.

This is the story of the wonder who is Ricochet, and how ADHD impacts his life and our family.

1

In the beginning

"Toto, I have a feeling we're not in Kansas anymore."
— *L. Frank Baum*

The day I had a son

When you set out to have children, you wish for a healthy and happy baby. You may hope for a particular gender, but you know either is great as long as the baby is healthy. Most expectant mothers have fleeting fears during pregnancy that their baby will be ill or disabled, but plan for a "normal" child unless someone warns them otherwise. I, of course, was no different.

With my first pregnancy, I was desperate to have a girl. I do mean *desperate*! I didn't have experience with little boys. This pacifist momma didn't have any interest in revving engines, guns, or explosives. I had an unhealthy fear that I would not know what to do with a boy. How would I relate to a boy? How would we bond? I knew I'd love my child, boy or girl, but I nearly broke out in hives at the mere thought of raising a boy.

A woman I worked with at the time, a single mother of two teen boys, told me time and time again that there is something very special about the bond between a boy and his mom. (Thanks for trying, Gwen, but it wasn't enough to allay my fears.) I pictured putting a girl in pretty dresses, with pigtails and bows in her hair. I imagined intuitively understanding her emotions and needs, such as how to support her through her first crush. The unknown of having my first child meant I needed the familiarity of a girl.

Thank goodness someone out there was listening! Warrior Girl was born full-term and beautiful, with all ten fingers, all ten toes, and a great set of lungs — a totally "normal" little girl. Her naturally busy persona, along with a six-month bout of colic, presented some challenges, but for the most part, being her momma came naturally.

Three years later, I found myself pregnant again, and just a handful of weeks into this pregnancy, I knew I was having a boy. (You can't conceive a girl when your husband is celebrating the Super Bowl win of his favorite team, can you?) My intuition was confirmed by ultrasound during my fifth month of pregnancy. While I was relieved the baby appeared to be developing normally, I was ripe with fear. I was convinced boys are trouble.

Once I knew Baby #2's gender for certain, I immersed myself in preparing for the arrival of a baby boy. I bought little blue onesies and rompers. My mom made a blue checkered quilt with a sailboat for his crib. I bought a new car seat, stroller, and bouncy seat because Warrior

Girl's hand-me-downs were too dainty for a boy. I was as ready as I could be for this unknown.

I was very sick while pregnant with Ricochet — I was showing after just six weeks, and my baby-bump ballooned to nearly full-term circumference by month six. I was huge, and my digestive system revolted. I had severe heartburn, and had to sleep sitting up for months. I lived on a diet of mostly milk products. I had a face full of acne like I'd never experienced, and I could barely get two hours of sleep at a time. I was the poster-child of miserable.

By thirty-seven weeks, my obstetrician estimated the baby would weigh nine or ten pounds at birth. From then on, at each of my weekly appointments, I begged her, "Get him out of me!" Each week I heard the same speech:

"You haven't made any progress toward beginning labor. Your baby boy just isn't ready to be born yet. If we induce now, without an emergent need, it will be more difficult for you and for the baby. We'll check again next week. I know you're miserable, but hang in there."

I heard that speech three weeks in a row. On the third week, I cried. I was so miserable and so ready to not be pregnant anymore. My obstetrician finally induced labor a week before my due date. However, being a stubborn male, Ricochet all but refused to come out. I labored nearly twice as long with him as with Warrior Girl.

My labor was not only long, but the last few hours were intensely difficult. For a time, my nurses couldn't find the baby's heartbeat, and I was on oxygen and vomiting as I pushed. Afterward, I was limp from exhaustion. I was so wiped out that I let them take Ricochet to the nursery for the night so I could get some rest.

A few hours later, I got out of bed to go to the bathroom. I took one step, first putting my weight on my right leg. Then I began to take a second step and realized that my left leg felt numb, completely dead. I fell to the floor the moment I put weight on it, jolting upon impact. I immediately freaked out, thinking my epidural had gone wrong and I was partially paralyzed. *Icing on the cake!* I thought, unable to hold back tears.

I later learned that the anesthesiologist had done a partial spinal block to fix the patchiness of my epidural, but no one had told me or warned me of its effects. Luckily, the epidural eventually wore off, and sensation returned to my leg several hours later.

Ricochet made his arrival in dramatic fashion. Definitely a boy! He was already turning my world upside down. I should have known then, life with him would always be dramatic. But he was a beautiful, healthy baby boy, and he loved his momma like only a son can.

Seeing signs

Newborn Ricochet and I bonded quickly. From day one, I felt that special mother-son connection my friend had told me about. I was hopelessly in love.

Ricochet's babyhood was pretty uneventful. He was generally healthy, although a little late to roll over, sit up, and crawl. In fact, he never really crawled, but pulled his body across the floor with his arms, like a soldier in boot camp drills. He wasn't so late with any of these milestones that his pediatrician was concerned, so I wasn't concerned either.

Ricochet was a quiet baby and toddler. He was easygoing, communicating more with a soft brush of my cheek or a bright smile on his face than by being vocal. His sister had been a difficult, rebellious toddler, but Ricochet was noticeably different. I loved having two children with completely opposite personalities. Warrior Girl was talkative, spunky, and always busy. Ricochet was gentle, soft-spoken, and laid back — until he suddenly wasn't!

One day in Ricochet's second or third year, I realized that he was talking incessantly. *That's new*, I thought, but I figured he was just taking cues from his motor-mouth sister, and didn't think much more about it. He seemed to be "coming alive." He was still sweet and gentle, but had much more spunk and energy and a lot more to say.

The first real clue that Ricochet's increasingly energetic pre-K behavior was caused by more than just his gender revealed itself in 2007, when we enrolled him in kindergarten.

The school meetings begin

Ricochet had not attended preschool, because his grandma was available to care for him while I worked. We knew he was pretty young to be starting kindergarten; he would not turn five until mid-October, but the school district's policy specified that any child who would turn five by October 16th was eligible to start. We could tell how intelligent and observant Ricochet was, even at the ages of three and four, so, despite his relative youth and lack of preschool experience, we were confident he was ready to start kindergarten.

Ricochet's kindergarten teacher, whom I'll call Ms. K (short for kindergarten), called me around 11:00 AM on the second day of school.

"Ms. Williams, we need to meet about Ricochet. Can you come in after school today?" she asked. She sounded exhausted.

"Of course!" I said. "I'll meet you in your classroom at three o'clock."

My mind raced for the next four hours. *What could we possibly need to talk about?* I wondered. *It's only the second day of school, for goodness' sake.* I signed in at the school office exactly at three o'clock and headed straight for the classroom — I couldn't wait any longer to know what this was about.

Ms. K began the meeting cordially as Ricochet played with some building blocks off in the corner of the classroom. "Thank you for coming in on short notice to meet with me. Ricochet is exhibiting troubling behaviors in the classroom."

"Okay," I said, figuring he was just a bit rambunctious as at home.

Ms. K continued, her tone less cordial. "He cannot even write his own name. He doesn't have any interest in reading at all. He was flailing his scissors so nonchalantly during an activity this morning that I was afraid he was going to hurt the students around him, so I had to take his scissors away. He talks and wiggles constantly.

"But, worst of all, this morning he stood up too fast when I was leaning over him from behind. He head-butted me really hard in the chin and knocked my glasses off my face. It hurt so bad that I cried. Ricochet must have more awareness of his surroundings. I'm pregnant, and he just can't continue to hurt me, or possibly others." An annoyed tone was woven through her words now.

I didn't know what to say. I'm sure I looked dumbfounded. I certainly felt that way.

"You have to teach him to control his body, and to focus on the task at hand," she continued. "He wasn't prepared for kindergarten, and now it's affecting our class."

It's only the second day of school! I shouted... in my head. I fought to rein in my shock before responding aloud.

"We'll be happy to work with Ricochet on some things at home," I concluded, and thanked her for her time.

I had been blindsided.

And the hits keep coming

Ricochet's school experience didn't improve after Ms. K and I had that first talk. Just when Ricochet was starting to learn Ms. K's expectations, she went on maternity leave and was gone for nearly three months. For Ricochet, having to get used to a substitute teacher was like starting the school year all over again. For me, it was déjà vu. The substitute sent home notes about Ricochet's inappropriate behavior nearly every day, just as Ms. K had.

"Ricochet is not staying on task."

"Ricochet will not sit still during carpet time."

"Ricochet is unaware of when he's in other children's personal space."

Blah, blah, blah. Yadda, yadda...

When Ms. K returned from maternity leave, she brought her infant daughter to school with her — *every day*. That bears repeating. The teacher had her newborn in the classroom with her all day, every day, for the rest of the school year. This classroom was tiny, packed full of play stations, bookcases, and tables, not to mention students. Yet, she laid her baby on a blanket on the floor, and repeatedly warned eighteen five-year-olds, "Watch out for the baby!"

Ricochet was told, "Slow down!", "Watch out!", and "Don't get that close to the baby!" dozens of times every day. I was distressed by the effect the baby's presence had on the classroom environment, but I never complained about it since no one else did. If I had a do-over, I sure would handle the situation differently! Ms. K continued to point her finger at Mr. T and me, saying we hadn't prepared Ricochet for school and didn't give him enough responsibilities at home; she held us wholly responsible for Ricochet's behavior. That left me bewildered — Ricochet was a smart kid, and isn't kindergarten the year of preparation anyway? Between the blame she was placing on us, and the constant negative feedback Ricochet was subjected to at school, I considered pulling him out about three-quarters of the way through the year. He could try kindergarten again the following fall, I thought. I didn't listen to my inner voice, though. I sure wish I had now.

During the summer that followed, I spent a lot of time thinking about how he'd struggled and worrying about the coming school year. The more I thought about it, the more convinced I became that the classroom environment, the teacher, and the loose culture of the charter school were to blame. These school issues weren't a problem with my sweet, intelligent Ricochet, or with his upbringing, I thought. *I can fix this!*

We pulled our kids from the charter school, which Warrior Girl had attended successfully for three years, and enrolled them in a mainstream public school the following academic year. That summer held within our normal, and I was confident Ricochet would hit his stride in first grade and everything would be great in the new school. But, just a couple of weeks into the school year, his teacher, whom I'll call Ms. Marvelous (because she was), started sending home reports about Ricochet's problem behaviors; he was not completing tasks, was unable to sustain focus, and was breaking classroom rules. I felt a sinking sensation in my gut. The problem hadn't been solely the kindergarten classroom or the kindergarten teacher, after all.

Something was going on with Ricochet. That realization was crushing.

I immersed myself in research. I was convinced that Ricochet's behaviors were clues to some underlying issue, and I was determined to figure out exactly what that issue was. My research led me to two possible conclusions: learning disabilities and ADHD. As I read more about both conditions, I became confident that Ricochet's problems stemmed from learning disabilities because he could sustain attention for certain activities. I took Ricochet straight to the pediatrician, and he was referred to a developmental specialist who could evaluate him for learning disabilities. I didn't give any serious thought to the possibility that Ricochet had ADHD.

Life is never what you expect, is it?

The day that changed all the others

The local children's outpatient center was big, intimidating, and scary that day. Giant wooden leaves hung from the ceiling, and paintings of cute bugs adorned the walls. The waiting area was designed to keep spirits up with bright colors and big windows to let the sun shine in. But on that day, it felt cavernous instead, and I felt as though I was about to be swallowed up. This was an ominous place for someone in this momma's shoes. I'd come here to find out what was wrong with my son.

I sat rigidly on the edge of my chair while I waited. I clutched my purse and stack of paperwork — the multiple questionnaires, samples of Ricochet's schoolwork, and notes from my research — tightly to my chest. I studied my fingernails and the floor's linear pattern, constructing the imminent appointment in my imagination. The doctor would ask Ricochet and me some questions. He'd watch Ricochet play. Then he'd give me a diagnosis. I'd leave armed with the knowledge necessary to help Ricochet succeed — to solve his problems in school.

It didn't turn out anything like I'd imagined.

After giving Ricochet a physical examination, conversing with him, and leading him through some activities to gage articulation, processing, and writing skills, the doctor turned to me, and said, "Ricochet has ADHD."

My mind became a jumbled mess. I couldn't follow what the doctor said next — all I heard were muffled sounds I couldn't make sense of. I checked out. My mind raced, trying to rationalize what I'd just been told. I thought back to what I'd read about ADHD.

Ricochet's life would be tragically altered, forever.

School would be impossible for him.

He would always feel sad and inferior.

I fought to keep myself together and not cry in front of this stranger, this matter-of-fact doctor. I held my breath and wished for time to stand still so I could catch up.

The doctor explained ADHD to my deaf ears and handed me five or six fact sheets. Then he said he wanted to prescribe a stimulant medication. I heard those words clearly somehow. They resonated like a gong, jolting me back to the present.

"I can't make that decision without talking to my husband," I told the doctor. I had just been told that my son has a neurological disorder. I needed time to process the information. It was way too soon to make that kind of decision. As the doctor continued talking, I focused on continuing to breathe. I nodded a lot and, when it was over, I got the heck out of there.

That night, Mr. T and I discussed the diagnosis and the recommended treatment. We tried to wrap our brains around the fact that ADHD meant Ricochet had a physiological difference in his brain that would likely always cause him to struggle with sustained attention, impulsivity, and hyperactive behavior.

"I will *NOT* give my child medication for bad behavior," Mr. T said through gritted teeth.

I could only nod. Tears flowed down my face and soaked my t-shirt. Mr. T and I agreed — we didn't want to "dope" our child.

Later, curled up in a chair in our bedroom, I was overcome with sorrow. I did little else for two days but sit there and think, think, think about ADHD. I grieved for the "normalcy" we'd just confirmed we'd never have. Eventually, I was able to rationally step back and reconsider the doctor's recommendation.

The signs were everywhere.
My long, difficult labor. The hours on Pitocin.[2] Ricochet's delays in reaching developmental milestones. His sudden talkativeness, difficulty controlling his body, lack of focus in a busy classroom,[3] and bad behavior from a sweet and kind kid. The signs really were everywhere, but I didn't know enough about ADHD to connect the dots. Each instance by itself can be something entirely different, random dots on a page. But, dots connected, it is a clear picture of ADHD — it's a clear picture of my son.

"If medication turns Ricochet into a zombie, or has any other unwanted side effects, we can stop using it, and look for other options, right?" I asked Mr. T. "Isn't anything worth a try for our son's happiness?" Mr. T agreed.

The next morning, just thirty-six hours after Ricochet's diagnosis, I called the doctor's office to request the prescription we'd been offered. I picked it up and filled it the next day.

The roller coaster begins

I felt a gnawing in my stomach all the way to the doctor's office to pick up Ricochet's prescription for

ADHD medication. Fear was hijacking my psyche. *What if it erases his personality? What if it accelerates his heart rate to a dangerous pace? What if it harms or, God forbid, kills my little boy?* These were rare possibilities, irrational fears really, but I couldn't stop them nonetheless. As we rode the elevator to the second floor of the medical building, Ricochet and Warrior Girl talked, talked, talked, and Ricochet ran circles around me in that tight little space. I considered what I'd give for quiet and stillness as I tried to remain sane.

I attempted to just grab the prescription and hurry back out of the doctor's office, but we had to wait for the nurse who was helping someone else. I already didn't want to be picking up a stimulant prescription for my barely six-year-old little boy — I certainly didn't want the uncomfortable task prolonged. We waited for what seemed like an eternity, then the nurse finally got to us.

"You need to know that the medicine may make his behavior worse before it improves. You call our office if you have questions or experience anything troubling," she said. "Do you have any questions for me now?"

My brow drooped lower, and I shook my head.

"Okay, sweetie. Remember, just call if you need anything," she said, her tone now candy-coated. She must have detected the terror in my eyes that my kids were, thankfully, too naive to see. "Happy Thanksgiving!"

Tomorrow's Thanksgiving! I thought. *How am I going to call for help when your office is closed for the next three days!* The holiday made starting medication that much more overwhelming.

We stopped at the pharmacy on the way home to fill the prescription. The doctor prescribed a medication that came in capsules because Ricochet hadn't learned to swallow pills yet. That allowed me to open the capsule and sprinkle the tiny granules inside over applesauce or yogurt. I had to pay $160 for it because we hadn't met our health insurance prescription deductible yet that year, adding insult to injury.

The next morning, I opened the medication capsule and sprinkled its contents on a spoonful of applesauce. Ricochet didn't ask about the little white granules in his applesauce; he just swallowed it down as if it were no big deal. I was certainly relieved to not have to figure out how to explain the medication to him in more detail on this first day. He knew that he was going to take medicine to help him make better choices and be more successful in school, and that was enough then. He finished his breakfast and ran upstairs to play in his bedroom. He was excited because his cousin was coming over and they loved to play together.

For the rest of the morning, I put my ear up to his chest every thirty minutes or so to be sure his heart rate wasn't too fast. I had read about that possibility, and kept envisioning his heartbeat racing so fast that he'd pass out, or worse. I was so nervous about it that I puttered around in my bedroom in order to be close to him.

I had given Ricochet the medicine at 10:10 AM. By 1:20 PM, I noticed that he was quick-tempered when things didn't go his way and very easily upset. When his cousin, Creative H, said she wanted a little "girl time" with Warrior Girl, he cried for a good twenty minutes.

He was so inconsolable that I scooped him up and sat on the step stool nearby, wrapped my arms tightly around him, and rocked him.

"It's okay. It's okay," I whispered, over and over again.

"It's not okay. It's not okay. It's not okay," he repeated as he sobbed.

I heard, "It's not okay you gave me this medication."

I kept holding him tight and rocked him back and forth, tears of guilt running down my face as I cried with him.

The nurse had warned me that Ricochet's behavior might get worse before it got better, especially if the dosage was too low. "He may have mood swings and be more aggressive as a side effect if the dose is not strong enough," she'd said. She had instructed me to give him two capsules after a couple days if we saw that type of behavior. By the time the medicine wore off on day one, we had battled through and survived at least three emotional meltdowns and half a dozen or more incidents of escalated aggression. I couldn't allow Ricochet or the rest of the family to live with these outbursts any longer than necessary. I planned to call the doctor's office to discuss increasing the dose if his mood didn't improve quickly.

When Ricochet had fallen asleep for the night, I breathed a huge sigh of relief, then went to my own bedroom to cry. It had been one of the most exhausting days of my life.

On Thanksgiving Day, day two of ADHD medication, Ricochet acted much the same as the day before — when his feelings were hurt he became aggressive, and then cried uncontrollably and called himself a "loser." Thankfully, he only had two of these episodes that day.

"You did a really good job at the movie theater today, Buddy. You were such a big boy," I said, as I tucked Ricochet into bed that night.

"No I wasn't, Momma. I was angry a lot," he said. "I don't like my medicine."

"We're going to keep adjusting how much medicine you take, and maybe what kind of medicine, until it is just right," I assured him. "I promise you won't always have extreme feelings you can't control."

Mr. T and I promised ourselves as much as well. If Ricochet wasn't significantly better the next day, we'd call the nurse and tell her we were ready to double the dose of his medication. Thankfully, Ricochet's mood and behavior improved a little bit each day, so, for the time being, we decided not to.

The third day he only had one episode of extreme emotion, and we didn't see any aggression at all. By an hour into medication on the fourth day, Ricochet was playing quietly in his room. He was content to play by himself, and was able to focus on one thing at a time — both firsts. He was finally happy and content, a welcome change.

School and medication

Ricochet's first day back at school after the Thanksgiving holiday was only his sixth day of taking medication to treat his ADHD. School had been rough all year with untreated ADHD, and adding the confusion of new medication was not a benefit at first. His nerves and emotions were raw from the added anxiety of being at school. With his teacher's blessing, I stayed in his classroom because I suspected it would be a tough adjustment, and Ricochet on medication at school was certainly a big unknown.

Ricochet was able to write and draw as instructed with a lot more clarity — a positive change I hadn't expected from medication. It was reassuring. However, anytime he made a mistake, he turned to me and said, "I'm such a loser! I can't do anything right!" His low self-esteem had been tough to watch over the fourteen months since that first day in kindergarten, but this was far more frequent and truly gut-wrenching for this momma.

After a couple of hours in the classroom with only one emotional outburst about having to make corrections on his writing, I asked Ricochet if I could go eat lunch with Warrior Girl's class and then come back to stay with him. Warrior Girl was feeling like Ricochet was the favorite child because he was requiring extra attention, so I wanted to show her that she's special to me, too. After fifteen minutes or so of angry glares and outright refusal to let me go, Ricochet smiled at me and told me it was okay if I ate lunch with Warrior Girl. That was the Ricochet I knew — he knew it would make his sister feel good, and he wanted that. That felt like good progress.

However, when I returned to his classroom less than an hour later, Ricochet was under his desk, clutching his coat as though it were his Blankie, and crying. He said he was upset because he missed me and he felt really nervous. It took a couple of minutes to coax him out. I sat on his tiny desk chair and held him, rubbing his back for a few minutes. Then I successfully redirected his attention to the activity his class was engaged in, the only thing that really broke him free during these emotional episodes. I stayed with him the rest of the day, and he did pretty well at school that afternoon.

He had some anger issues after school, though. We stopped at Grandma's house on the way home where he got mad at Warrior Girl and threw a large beanbag into Grandma's antique mirror. Later, when we were back at home and doing homework, he wrote his "9" backward. I asked him to erase it and try again, something I asked at least once every time we worked on his homework. He threw his pencil at the wall, then made a gun with his fingers and stuck it in my face, while snarling. This type of behavior had never occurred before starting the medication, not even once.

"You're in time out," I declared. "You can choose to finish your work or not while in time out." I set the kitchen timer and walked away.

By the time his five time-out minutes were finished, he had completed his math. He also apologized to me for the incident with great remorse. What confused me most about these two episodes was that his medication should have worn off long before that time. I called the developmental specialist's office the next morning and spoke with a nurse about the changes in Ricochet's moods and behavior.

"He's having some wild mood swings and episodes of anxiety, even after I thought his medication would have worn off," I explained. "Are these signs that we should double his dosage to 20 mg?"

She spoke with Ricochet's doctor and called me back that afternoon. "If you are seeing some positive changes in focus and behavior, try increasing the dosage. If not, the doctor wants to switch him to a different stimulant."

"I've definitely seen Ricochet focus more and fidget less at times. His assistant teacher told me how proud she is of his writing since starting medication, too. Let's try the 20 mg dosage to see if there's an improvement before changing medications and starting from scratch again," I said. I wasn't ecstatic about throwing out the $160 initial prescription, but I wasn't about to put a price on the wellbeing of my son either.

Here we go again

After two weeks on the 20 mg dose, a pattern emerged. According to Ms. Marvelous, Ricochet was calm, attentive, and mostly on task up until about one o'clock, but was having trouble controlling his emotions the rest of the school day. We concluded that the medication was wearing off while Ricochet was still in school, so he was having trouble controlling his emotions after that time.

His doctor decided it was time to try something different, since there was not a longer-acting version of that particular stimulant, and prescribed a medication from the amphetamine class, Medication #2.

Now, Ricochet was constantly angry and lashing out over the smallest things, he lost his train of thought mid-sentence, his anxiety was through the roof, and he barely ate a thing all day. We realized before he'd been on it a full week that it was not the right type of medication for Ricochet. The original medication was much better, despite its problems, so I called the doctor and asked if we could switch back to it and try to overcome the negatives he was experiencing on Medication #1. After all, he had only been on the original medication two weeks — maybe that hadn't been enough time to fairly evaluate its efficacy. The doctor agreed, and Ricochet went back on the 20 mg dose of Medication #1.

Back to square one

The medication originally prescribed for Ricochet's ADHD didn't seem to work as well the second time around. I was stunned. *How could that be?* I wondered. The first day was okay, but on the second, the principal called me two hours before the end of the school day.

"Ms. Williams?" she asked.

It's never good when someone calls me during the school day and calls me Ms. Williams, I thought. "Yes?"

"Ricochet is having a rough day at school today. He has been yelling and crying for quite a while over a cause we can't pinpoint. I took him from the classroom to take a walk with me, I asked him to be my helper, but nothing consoles him. Do you want to go ahead and pick him up? The only thing that has quieted him is to tell him his mom might pick him up early since he's not feeling well." She was calm and matter-of-fact, but I heard compassion in her tone as well.

He had an emotional meltdown at school. It was hard to tell what was going on with Ricochet. It was the last day of school before the two-week holiday break, and the schedule was completely different from the typical school day, so the anxiety of not knowing what to expect might

46

have wreaked havoc on his emotions. Or, it could be related to the medicine. I called Ricochet's doctor with an update.

Switching back to the original medication was like starting at square one again, with his difficulty adjusting apparent through mood swings. I came to realize that, not only does Ricochet's body need time to chemically adjust to the medication, but he needs time to adjust mentally and emotionally with each change as well.

Based on Ricochet's first trial of this medication, as well as the previous day's outburst at school, the doctor thought Ricochet was experiencing a rebound effect as the medication wore off — a period of thirty minutes to a couple of hours where the medication is diminishing and troublesome behaviors escalate. He added a "booster" dose, both to soften the rebound and to get Ricochet through the school day. The booster was in pill form and had to be swallowed, something Ricochet had never done before. I put it in the middle of a spoonful of applesauce and it went right down without issue.

The booster didn't have the desired effect. Soon, the entire family would scatter when Ricochet came near, like the townspeople who frantically dispersed when Godzilla approached. That is so very sad, but it was true. His anger was volatile and unpredictable. He began to employ a very mean stare to get what he wanted — something he'd perfected since starting ADHD medication. I felt like he was trying to control me, and his tone of actions was frightening.

Determined not to be bullied, I went about my day. I took the kids with me, running errands and picking up last minute items for Christmas. Trouble started at the very first store. Despite being six years old, Ricochet wanted to ride in a shopping cart so he could ward off boredom by playing his Nintendo. No carts were available. Ricochet was angry from the start.

"You just don't want me to ride in a cart, *Mom*!" He called me "Mom" instead of the more endearing "Momma" when he was mad at me.

"What am I supposed to do, Buddy?" I replied. "You saw that there are no shopping carts available."

"You could find one if you wanted to. You just don't want me to have a cart so I can't play my game." He folded his arms tightly against his chest and blew a deep puff of air through his throat.

"We are honestly only going to be in this store less than five minutes," I said. "I promise I'll be sure you get a cart at our next stop, and we will go home right after that."

He continued to show his disgust with me, but quit arguing, and I finished my shopping in under five minutes, as promised. *Whew! I side-stepped a nasty scene, somehow!* I took his hand as we walked out the door.

Halfway to the car, Ricochet snapped. He screamed and kicked at me, at a level of rage I hadn't seen from him before. I held his hand tighter, alert to the danger a parking lot meltdown could entail.

"Let go of my hand!" he screamed. There were a lot of people in the parking lot, and most of them stopped in their tracks.

"I don't want to be part of this family anymore! I'm not part of this family! You don't love me! Let go of me. Let go of meeeeeee!"

He flung his body in the opposite direction of mine repeatedly, attempting to use all his strength to try to break free of me and take off running. It was all I could do to physically sustain my grip on him and inch toward our car. The stares of onlookers were piercing, and I became overwhelmed with panic.

"Please look right here in my eyes so I can talk to you for just a second," I pleaded. "A lot of people are staring at us because they are concerned about you. It sounds to them like I am hurting you. When people think a child is being hurt, they usually call the police. If the police come, they could think Momma is a bad mom to you and take you away from our family. I don't want that, and I know you don't either. That would be really, really bad. Please come to the car calmly now and then you can tell me how you feel."

"Fine!" he shouted. I kept a tight grip on him until he was in the car, glancing down to be sure the child lock was on before I closed and locked his door. My arms were already aching from the unaccustomed effort as I drove away.

Most moms would cut their losses and head for home without one thought of stopping on the way. I wasn't that sensible yet. *ADHD is not going to ruin my day. I'm not wasting gas to take him home and come back out later. Surely the drama is over for the day.* I hadn't yet learned that sometimes you do have to cut your losses, or you'll potentially magnify them tenfold instead.

Ricochet did much better at the second store, but he rode in a shopping cart and played his Nintendo, precisely what he had wanted in the first place. The ADHD medication had not stopped this crazy roller coaster ride of rapidly changing emotions yet.

Time for a change

Ricochet continued on the original medicine for almost a month, enough time to effectively evaluate its efficacy. His grand mood swings and episodes of extreme anger and aggression persisted. One evening, I finally noticed the very obstinate behavior was happening late in the afternoon every day.

Ricochet had been refusing to do his homework daily.

"This math worksheet is stupid! It's too hard. I can't do it," he grumbled.

"What is hard about it? I'm happy to help you with your math."

"No! I'm not doing it! It's stupid!" He was yelling very close to my face now.

"You need to do your homework, and we will do it together," I said calmly. "Now, take a breath and turn around here to the table, and let's get started."

He answered by shoving me and punching me. That was when I snapped.

"Go to your room right now! Get in there and don't come out until you're calm and ready to apologize. You will not treat your mother this way!" Calm had left the building.

He ran halfway up the stairs, then turned toward me and chucked his pencil down the corridor straight toward my face. He was lucky that I quickly ducked and dodged the bullet. He was also lucky he was already on his way to his room. His bedroom door slammed a couple of seconds later.

I started cooking dinner in the kitchen, right at the foot of the stairs. I contemplated how he was deliberately doing the opposite of everything I wanted. I became afraid that he'd open his bedroom window, three stories up, because we had reminded him again and again how dangerous it would be to open it. It was the first time since he was a toddler that I feared he would make a stupid choice and get hurt. This was the first week of his six years on the earth that he had punched me or thrown anything at me with malice. I couldn't accept this Ricochet-on-Medication, despite the fact that his schoolwork had improved significantly. I wanted my sweet and kind boy back. I wanted this demon-child to go away.

I dropped what I was doing and ran up to Ricochet's bedroom. My intent was to be sure he wasn't hurting himself, but I also hoped to finally calm him down. I opened his bedroom door and took a quick survey of the room. *Phew!* He had not opened any windows.

"Buddy, come sit next to me on your bed. I just want to talk to you," I said. I could tell he was already starting to calm down, because he came right over willingly and sat down gently.

"I don't want homework to make us fight," I explained. "I know it's hard for you, but we can work together. Why did you get so upset about doing your worksheet?"

Whining, he said, "It's too long. It's way too much for me to do. It will take a million weeks!" He laid his head on my arm. "Homework is too hard for me! I'm just a stupid jerk!"

"You are not stupid, and you are most definitely not a jerk! You are a sweet and kind boy who sometimes can't control how he shows anger," I said as I stroked his head softly. "I'm going to call your doctor and ask for different medicine. I will keep working on that until you can be yourself, I promise."

I held on to him for a little while longer, wishing I could simply love all his struggles away. After a couple of minutes of silence, he lifted his head and looked up at me with those sparkly blue eyes that always melt my heart. "I'm sorry I was mean to you, Momma."

"I know, Buddy. Momma knows you don't mean it."

I did not mention homework again that night, and he never completed that math worksheet — it wasn't worth it.

I walked downstairs and left a voice-mail at the doctor's office for the nurses to pick up first thing the next morning — being a violent, raging six-year-old abuser was not a fair trade for being able to focus and do school work effectively. That was the last day Ricochet took that medicine.

Struggling to make lemonade

When life gives you lemons, you make lemonade, right?

In 2004, Mr. T was diagnosed with Ankylosing Spondilitis (AS), an autoimmune disorder that causes joint pain similar to arthritis but with possible joint fusion. We read as much as we could about the diagnosis, learned the disease can be managed and is not fatal, and decided to approach it as an obstacle, not the end of the world. Some days AS really sucks, but tomorrow can be better.

When the Real Estate market tanked and my income started to dry up in 2009, I recognized it was a blessing because it allowed me the time and flexibility to work with Ricochet, his school, and his doctors to get to the root of his school problems and find some resolution.

When Ricochet was diagnosed with ADHD, I let grief consume me for a couple of days, and then said to myself, "It could be worse." I could reflect on these dark clouds and find the silver lining. Tough as some obstacles have been to accept, I've never disputed that it can always be worse.

Now, we'd been given some very sour lemons in the form of ADHD medication side effects. I was really struggling to make something good out of this medication mess, though. But I was "testing" neurological medications on my young child, for goodness sake! How do you sweeten that?

We had tried and failed with two different stimulant medications at this point — each change sparked by the fact that the medications were causing serious anger, violence, and rage in Ricochet in the afternoons. Each time we started a new medication (or returned to one previously tried), I pegged all my hopes on that medication being "the one" for Ricochet. The one that would greatly improve his focus and ability at school. The one that would keep him positive and happy. The one that would not cause him to physically and mentally abuse me each afternoon. The one that would help with ADHD symptoms and return my kind, sweet Momma's boy.

Each time we changed his medicine or dosage, I fell very hard from those high hopes I was perched on. I was still searching for the secret to "fixing" my little boy. I wanted to erase his ADHD and all his struggles.

However, I knew this journey was hard and that it took time to discover success. It was excruciating to give my son a medication each morning that I knew created a personality I couldn't tolerate and a set of emotions my son would grieve for each evening. But I held my breath, gave him his pill, and climbed back up on those hopes again. This momma was going to find a way to make life better for her son.

Mr. T and I gave each new medication a few days to see if his aggressive and/or emotional episodes would subside when his body and mind adjusted. We agreed to stop a medication if Ricochet had the same rages each day for three days; we would know then it was not the one. We had already stopped a medication twice by these guidelines, and now it was time for Medication #3 and a whole new batch of unknowns.

Yep, again.

The first day on Medication #3, a long-acting methylphenidate used to treat ADHD, was the worst day of our medication trials up to that point. This medication turned my sweet son into a two-legged raging horror. I questioned the medication change. I considered that he might be one of the 20% who see no benefits from stimulants. I questioned my ability to effectively parent a child with ADHD. I certainly questioned our decision to give him medication in the first place. I was on edge all day, then sat in my room and cried at night, when Ricochet was finally asleep and at peace.

I was sure the second day of Medication #3 would be the last day for this pill. Success at school was not worth changing our child's essence.

I picked him up from school and asked how his day was, as I always did. Then I braced myself.

"Fantastic!" he said. "I finished all my work, and I felt like myself today."

My heart leapt.

He did so great at school that day, in fact, his assistant teacher sent me an email explaining that Ricochet was so quiet and on task she almost forgot he was there. *Yay Ricochet!*

We headed over to my sister, Auntie's house so Ricochet could play with Creative H for about forty-five minutes until we had to pick up Warrior Girl from an after-school club. Ricochet was a perfect gentleman and got ready to leave the first time I asked him to. We picked up Warrior Girl and headed home.

"I can't believe the snow melted already," he said in a soft voice from the backseat. "I want to play in the snow and have a snowball fight with Warrior Girl."

"I'm sorry, Buddy. It did melt fast, didn't it?" I saw him nodding in agreement as I glanced at his face in the rearview mirror. "Next time it snows, I will be sure you get a chance to play in it." I held my breath and waited for him to get upset.

"Okay, Momma."

That's it? He accepts that? Uh, wow! He is having an awesome day!

His little mind kept buzzing though, and soon he was on to another plan.

"From now on, I'm going to ride my bike to school," he said excitedly.

This plan would take some perseverance for sure, since we lived a mile *up* a gravel mountain road and another two miles on a winding, busy road from his school. Not to mention, he didn't know how to ride his bike on his own yet! I didn't want to crush his plans twice in a row, but I had to be honest with him — this one was not going to work for me, and it definitely wasn't going to work for him either.

About the time I was attempting to let him down easy on his plan to bike to school, we were halfway up the mountain to our house, and he began to notice there was still some snow higher up. Boy, was he excited! In an effort to be a fun momma — a real effort to step into his shoes and see things from his perspective, and be sensitive to the fact that he was trying to adjust to a mind-altering medication — I struck a deal with my two little people.

"I'll make a deal with you," I explained to them. "There are fifteen minutes until our four o'clock homework time. We can walk down the drive to the closest patch of snow, and you can play in the snow for fifteen minutes. But, you have to promise to go inside and do your homework as soon as those fifteen minutes are up. Deal?"

"Deal!" they exclaimed in unison.

Ricochet ran into the house to put on his mittens, and came out wearing his bike helmet, too — he hadn't given up on biking yet. Off we skipped in search of some un-melted snow.

His behavior and mood were great, but I couldn't help but brace myself for the ticking time bomb I was pretty sure was still set to detonate. I gave a two-minute warning before time was up. No complaints.

"Alright! Time is up. We have to go inside and do homework now," I called, and then held my breath. The only thing I could hear were little feet shuffling up the gravel drive. Not one complaint about having to quit playing or doing homework. I'm pretty sure I heard angels singing in chorus.

Ricochet came in the front door and took his wet shoes off right there, without being asked. Then he hung his coat up, again, without being asked. You could have scraped me off the floor by this point, but I just kept observing discreetly. He grabbed his homework folder out of his backpack and headed toward the kitchen table. And, as monumental as all those things were for him already, he proceeded to take his homework out of the folder and start writing his vocabulary sentences all by himself! He completed his homework without me begging, arguing, and sitting right next to him. In fact, he had very little input from me at all. This was colossally huge!

The rest of the day, I think I floated on a cloud of pure elation. I was back up high on all the hopes I had for Ricochet. I could see the potential success and happiness he so deserved. I knew there would still be bumps in the road, probably lots of them, but I also now knew medication could work for him. I reveled in the relief for a while. I needed this break!

Time to get serious about this ADHD

At every appointment with Ricochet's developmental specialist, he always recommended two services: occupational therapy (OT) and family psychotherapy. I didn't give much thought to psychotherapy at the time — parenting a child with ADHD was rough, but I was handling it quite well, I thought. Plus, our insurance wouldn't cover the first $5,000 of mental health visits each year, so we basically had no insurance to cover the weekly $200 therapy visits.

Occupational therapy was different in my mind, though. I had been reading a lot about ADHD and sensory issues, and OT was always recommended for children with these disabilities. Now that he was settled with an effective medication, it was time to add some of these services. We started with OT since there was an entire OT department in the behavioral and developmental health practice we then frequented. I called and set up the appointment, then counted down the days. I was eager to see what benefits OT might offer Ricochet.

The OT evaluation was very revealing, as he had difficulty with many of the tasks. However, one really stuck with me — he couldn't transfer words from a sheet posted just a few feet in front of him to the paper on the desk where he was seated. He looked up constantly, kept losing his place, and made many mistakes in the very little he managed to copy down. I knew his handwriting was a huge challenge, but this was different, an additional hurdle.

The forty-minute evaluation concluded, and the therapist looked at me, and said, "He can definitely benefit from OT. There's a lot we should work on."

I expected that.

I received the therapist's report in the mail a few weeks later, and it offered a lot of detail about Ricochet's struggles.

Here is the OT evaluation report in a nutshell:

1. Average fine motor skills—that shocked me because Ricochet has a terrible time with handwriting.
2. Above average manual dexterity
3. Below average bilateral coordination, repeating patterns with his arms and legs
4. Poor concept of spacing and placement in handwriting
5. Overall typical performance in sensory areas, but needs definite improvement in auditory, vestibular (movement), behavioral, and emotional sensory responses

I was shocked to learn that Ricochet had average fine motor skills and above average manual dexterity because of his immense struggle with handwriting. The rest was expected.

She outlined goals for a six-month therapy program:

1. Utilize a tripod grasp with engaged thumb to correctly write his name, with use of lowercase letters
2. Copy an age-appropriate sentence with spacing between words, minimal verbal cues for accuracy

That sounded great, and I felt comfortable with this therapist and her services. However, even with insurance coverage, we couldn't afford the $200 a month in copays to see her weekly, as she recommended. I had asked the school to evaluate Ricochet for special services back before his diagnosis, and I was still waiting to find out if they would provide some OT at school. I told the evaluating OT that I'd wait to see what the school would provide, then bring him in to see her to fill in the gaps. I was really depending on the school to step up and provide the services Ricochet needed for academic success.

My New Motherhood

So there I was, now fully immersed in a new motherhood. A world of doctor appointments, behavioral therapy and occupational therapy, medication trials, Special Education laws, school accommodations, dietary changes, guilt, anxiety, and even grief. I hadn't had any training for this motherhood, and it didn't come so naturally. I didn't expect to hold this job, nor, frankly, did I even want it. But this job, this new motherhood, came with Ricochet, and it was here to stay.

Mothering a child with ADHD is indisputably more difficult than mothering a neurotypical child. It's downright exhausting. There are so many more appointments, so many more worries, so much more stress. This new motherhood can feel like trial by fire, but it made me a stronger, more compassionate person right from the start. For that, I am grateful.

2
Learning to Cope

"A goal without a plan is just a wish."
— *Antoine de Saint-Exupéry*

The proudest momma in the room

Once Ricochet's developmental issues were undeniable, I resolved to accept that his grades wouldn't be great and he'd likely never achieve an academic award at school. However, halfway through his first-grade year, he brought home an invitation that read, "Your child will be receiving an award. Please join us." *What? That can't be right.* While Ricochet was intelligent enough to earn an academic achievement award, his school performance was mediocre at best due to his ADHD. Warrior Girl was getting an award in an upper-grade ceremony just before, so I attended both, but I figured Ricochet must be getting an attendance award, or something like that.

The academic awards ceremonies were not the most pleasant hours of my kids' elementary days. The room was not big enough for most events and was really dark, even with the lights on. There weren't any chairs in their little auditorium, just carpet-covered concrete risers that were as comfortable as sitting on, well, concrete. And it was always hot. Very hot. But I always attended.

I sat in the auditorium across the room from where Ricochet sat with his classmates, fanning myself with the program. I observed his behavior throughout the ceremony. I always watched his behavior in different scenarios to analyze how well his medication was working. He sat very still, but was a little disengaged — he did not clap with the audience, and he sat with his knees pulled up to his chest the entire time. He seemed uncomfortable within that environment. He liked to know what to expect, and this was a new situation for him. The ceremony was almost over when I heard:

"Academic Growth Award, Ricochet Williams." His teacher announced his name, for an academic award! I had never been so happy to be wrong!

Ricochet came alive! A big smile lit up his face as he leapt down the stairs and onto the stage. I couldn't hold back the tears. I clapped so hard that my palms literally stung. My boy was beaming up on that stage! *That's my son!* The assistant principal handed Ricochet the certificate and shook his hand. This handshake was quite ironic, since he was receiving an award from the man whose office he had frequented over the prior five months. I know the assistant principal was proud to be presenting him an award for those very same reasons, too.

Ms. Marvelous recognized how much he had improved that school year, despite not being a great reader and still struggling with his handwriting and his ADHD. *Can I say it again? It never gets old. My son, who has ADHD and possibly additional learning disabilities, received an academic award!* I was floating again. I was proud to have my children in a school, a mainstream public school nonetheless, that was willing to recognize students of all needs and capabilities for the best in themselves, not just the best in the group.

His teachers deserved high praise as well — his academic improvement was mostly a credit to the two of them. From the very beginning, they cared for him despite his behavior. They recognized his differences and adjusted his learning environment just for him, and they gave Ricochet high praise for the smallest positive behavior and improvement. These teachers had such open hearts and open minds for their students, and it made all the difference in the world for a student like Ricochet. Saying, "Thank you" would never be enough.

Changing my compass

It didn't take long for the excitement to wear off. I had been packing around a ho-hum, woe-is-me demeanor since Ricochet's school struggles began; it was heavy and cumbersome. Constantly feeling sad, defeated, and like a complete parenting failure was as exhausting as trying to keep up with my clinically-hyperactive six-year-old. Together they multiplied. It was time for a new frame of reference.

It was now February 2009, two-thirds of the way through Ricochet's first grade year. He was still doing well on Medicine #3. His classroom teachers made sure he felt comfortable and successful in their classroom.

While his writing troubles continued to weigh heavily on me, he had made a tremendous amount of progress in a matter of five months — I finally realized it was time I celebrated that for a bit, instead of continuing to strive for perfection with blinders on.

Like anyone, I wanted to be happy. I needed to put on some rose-colored glasses. Not the kind that distort and make everything look rosy when it's not, but the kind that add a little punch of color to life and remind us to stop and smell the roses. In my quest for optimism, I read books and articles on being happy and finding your bliss. I began to look for the silver lining, the "good" in every situation first, before addressing the "bad."

I had a brutal anxiety of the unknown. I was constantly trying to predict the future without the capability to do so. Fear was playing the biggest role in how I felt about ADHD. My number one priority to achieve optimism and some renewed happiness had to be squelching my fear.

The trick was not to let fear be my compass. I needed to focus on the goal — the positive outcome we desired — when making decisions, not the target of avoidance.

How was I going to change my compass? Dr. Edward Hallowell, famed author on ADHD, teaches parents it's all about identifying the mirror traits of each ADHD characteristic. For example, the ADHD characteristic of distractibility; the positive mirror-trait to that is curiosity, a drive to discover and learn more. How about stubbornness and hyper-focus? That can also be viewed positively as determination and persistence, more traits of a successful individual.

Choosing optimism was actually my key to overcoming fear, which was my key to maintaining a naturally optimistic outlook. I made a concerted effort to constantly re-route my thoughts to the positive side of things. I would raise unhappy children if I only taught them that life is hard — I knew I had to teach the part about making lemonade, too.

Here's the positive flip-side of this Momma's ADHD-related fears:

~~I'm afraid I am not making the right treatment decisions for my son.~~
I'm making educated, thoughtful decisions on behalf of my son.

~~I'm afraid I'm harming him giving him medication.~~
I sought the advice of medical professionals who know more about medications than I, and medication is a tremendous positive influence on Ricochet's daily life.

~~I'm afraid there's some great treatment or therapy out there that I don't have the opportunity to provide.~~
I'm reading and researching ADHD daily, and I am doing much more for Ricochet than would have been done for him twenty years ago. I'm a strong advocate for my son.

~~I'm afraid my son won't have friends.~~
Having a few close friends is much more rewarding than popularity and an army of friendly acquaintances.

~~I'm afraid my son will be made fun of.~~
I don't have ADHD, and kids made fun of my name relentlessly throughout my childhood. Kids will be mean if they want to, with or without ammunition. I'll help

Ricochet learn funny and harmless come-backs to silence bullies.

~~I'm afraid my son will struggle with or fail in school.~~ I'm advocating for the best education for my son. I will not let him fail, but grades aren't everything.

~~I'm afraid my son will be punished for things he just can't help.~~ I'll educate friends, family, and teachers about ADHD, and help them understand that some behaviors are out of his control. I'll educate myself about creative ways to control those behaviors and share those insights.

~~I'm afraid my son will feel inferior and have low self-confidence/self-esteem.~~ I'll continue to encourage Ricochet. I'll praise his accomplishments and strengths and pay as little attention as possible to his deficits.

~~I'm afraid my son will still need ADHD medications when he's a teen.~~ I will accept that medication can help my son live a happy and successful life.

~~I'm afraid my son will have difficulty with relationships.~~ I'll pattern and teach relationship management skills.

~~I'm afraid my son will have difficulty keeping a job.~~ I'll help Ricochet discover, develop, and nurture his talents so he will be doing something he loves for a career.

~~I'm afraid my son will bounce around aimlessly in life and never feel like he "fits."~~ I'll continue to teach Ricochet coping skills and the structure necessary to manage his ADHD.

Writing a corresponding positive answer to each of my fears really helped to reduce their significance. Some were difficult, I won't lie — I'm still terrified of him driving.

Just getting out of bed each morning and reminding myself out loud that today will be a good day went a long way to keeping my compass pointed toward gratitude. I may not have been a superhero mom, but I was a strong and determined advocate for my kids, ADHD or not, and that meant a lot. I worked hard to point my compass toward gratitude.

Yet again

After only six weeks on Medication #3, Ricochet startled me with a revelation when he jumped in my car after school.

I always immediately asked, "How was your day, Buddy?"

"I can't follow directions and behave in school anymore. I'm getting in trouble a lot, and I don't like that," he whined (not that I could blame him).

This was not at all what I wanted or expected to hear. I assumed it was just a rough patch for some reason. I planned to pay closer attention to when and what he was eating and how much sleep he was getting to see if I could figure out the reason his medicine was now failing him. When we arrived home, there was an email from Ricochet's teacher waiting in my inbox. She said Ricochet had regressed back to a lot of his pre-medication behaviors — the reward system wasn't motivating him anymore, he was spending a lot of the day on the floor under his desk, he was chewing incessantly again, he needed supervision to get any work accomplished, and now he was also rocking back and forth quite a bit, a behavior we had not seen before.

I had noticed Ricochet's behavior at home was a little off in the days before, too, but I ignored it because I didn't want to see it.

I was devastated. He was finally doing so well — really, really well. He had tried many medications that made his ADHD worse instead of better, and Medication #3 finally revealed his true potential. Now, after just six short weeks, the medicine didn't seem to be working.

My first inclination was to dissect the week and look for potential clues. Did I give him food with artificial colors or preservatives, or over-the-counter medication that could have affected his ADHD medicine? Was I giving it to him after he ate breakfast when I should give it to him before? The loss of efficacy wasn't caused by a growth spurt, because he hadn't grown since starting medication; he'd actually lost five pounds. I needed to know what I'd done to cause this medication failure so I could fix it. I needed the medicine to work for Ricochet. I wanted him to do well!

I didn't even consider that he could have grown tolerant to the stimulant, especially in such a short time. If that were the case, he'd be on the maximum dose before his seventh birthday. I was not okay with that. Yet, I wasn't okay with this family destruction either — it was hard on everyone in the family when Ricochet didn't have effective ADHD treatment, including Ricochet.

The sibling effect

The extra attention paid to Ricochet was really bothering Warrior Girl, now almost ten. Mr. T and I had noticed many changes in her since Ricochet began school the year before — really, since he began doing poorly in school that year. She was more jealous of attention paid to Ricochet, as well as protective and anxious.

I certainly didn't blame all of these things on the ADHD factor. The transition to fourth grade, coupled with the accountability introduced that year, threw her off kilter, not to mention changing schools and leaving her friends. You didn't hear me complaining that she was protective of her brother. That made me happy because they didn't always get along so well. I welcomed her protective nature, as long as it didn't become obsessive, as it had been in her preschool years when she was constantly mother hen, attempting to keep him out of trouble.

I couldn't really blame her for being jealous of the extra attention Ricochet received. I was not going to feel guilty about it, either. He was really struggling and needed the extra help. I certainly wasn't neglecting her, despite her sometimes steadfast belief to the contrary. That was precisely why I made a point to have a special day with her.

She had been feverishly saving her chore money to build a stuffed dog at Build-a-Bear Workshop, so we chose that for our inaugural girls-only outing and made a day of it. We had lunch together at the mall, built her dog, and even did a little shopping.

Her favorite part of the day was not having her brother around. My favorite part was us two girls in the dressing room, trying on clothes. It was pretty cool to try on clothes with my daughter, despite the fact that I usually loathe the activity. This was monumental because it was the first time she seemed to enjoy clothes shopping, yet a bittersweet reminder of just how fast she was growing up, too.

Her anxiety was now troublesome as well, but I couldn't fully pin it on her brother's ADHD. In fact, I felt more certain it was not a direct result of the extra attention paid to her brother — part of it came from changing schools and from walking the line with puberty. She sometimes cried in school and got a stomachache for what often seemed like no reason. I couldn't figure out how to help her stop sweating the small stuff. Teaching gratitude to a tween was like trying to climb an icy mountain in stilettos!

How would I strike a balance with one special needs kid and one (mostly) neurotypical kid? How could I help the sibling grow from her special family dynamic instead of suffer from it? I wish I had answers but knew more girls-only days were a good start.

When it's the parent who rebels

Ricochet was obsessed with money. He went around the house checking everywhere he could think to look for spare coins, even in my wallet. He wanted everything and knew money was the magic solution to that ill. Money would always motivate Ricochet, and it was time I took advantage of that.

Reward and token systems are all the rage among ADHD experts. Dr. Russell Barkley suggests a token system in his book, *Taking Charge of ADHD*. His system rewards the child for good behaviors with tokens in their bank, and punishes by removing tokens. All activities the child wants to do are assigned a token value. *All* activities — TV watching, computer time, outside play, the works. There are no freebies in Dr. Barkley's system other than food, shelter, and love. While I think this system is smart on many levels (teaches handling money, budgeting, saving, earning things, etc.), I was not about to try it — out of fear. I had inadvertently let screen time become an entitlement in my children's minds, not privileges to be earned. I did limit them, but I had never made them earn these activities. Now, I feared anarchy.

I discovered a visual quarter system I felt might work for us. Paper quarters were stuck onto a posted chart for the child to visually see how they were doing. The theory was, when they saw all those quarters on their chart, they were motivated to make good behavior choices in order to earn more. That could work for my money-obsessed six-year-old!

I got to work right away printing dozens of quarters and cutting out the tiny circles by hand. I affixed a Velcro dot to the back of each. I then created a "$5" page for each child: it had five squares that equal $1, each square with four Velcro dots for quarters. Once the page was full of quarters, they put a $5 bill in their pouch affixed to their chart and cleared the quarters to begin again.

I originally implemented the quarter system for chores, still not forcing them to earn privileges. It was hard enough to keep up with behavior modification systems without turning our worlds upside down in addition. I had to keep the play money put up — Ricochet slyly added a $5 bill to his pouch when he put his first earned quarter, for setting the table, on his chart. He was smart and sneaky like that!

I planned to add bonuses for good behavior and fines for things like hitting each other, which was a daily occurrence then. I hoped to have the gumption to have them earn privileges they felt entitled to one day as well. Motivating desirable behavior was an improvement starting out, and I'd take as much of that as I could get. Gaining control of behavior was a marathon, not a sprint.

An epic snowball fight

One of the few times Ricochet and Warrior Girl got along then was when there was snow. They were always willing to go outside together when snow blanketed the ground, and this crisp winter day was no exception. I watched their fun below from the warmth of the indoors. I had stopped thinking snow was fun the first time I drove in it — it's beautiful, but I don't desire to be out in it.

The kids were using Mr. T's car as a barricade from potential snowball attack, one crouched down hiding on each side. They'd each scoop up a handful of snow, almost in unison, and pack it into a ball. Then the taunts and giggles began.

"I'm gonna get you!"

"I've got a really good snowball."

"Come out, come out, wherever you are!"

It would be as long as a couple of minutes after arming before one of them would move to begin their attack. It was so fun to watch from above and see one kid finally start to make a move, the other oblivious. Once snow crunching underfoot was audible, they both jumped up and ran after each other, usually in a circle around the car, like a mad cat and mouse chase. It was silly, but fun.

When we lived in the house on the mountain, my parents lived across the street from us. Papaw had spotted the snowball fight and prepared to get in on the fun. As he crested the hill of our long and curvy driveway, he bent down, scooped up a healthy handful of snow, and packed it into ammunition. The kids were oblivious to his presence until he hit Ricochet in the back with that first snowball. Game on!

When I saw Papaw approaching, I put on my coat and hat, grabbed my camera, and raced outside. I knew this was going to be a monumental snowball fight full of laughter and joy, and I wanted to capture those memories. I planted myself on the sidelines between Team Williams and Team Papaw.

Papaw was successful at launching his snowballs down the driveway to reach the kids from his position on the crest. Warrior Girl was content with a few reaching the target, i.e. Papaw, without much movement, so they each kept their respective posts for the most part, Papaw high and Warrior Girl down low.

However, Ricochet employed every strategy he could come up with to win this fight for Team Williams. He crouched down at the lowest end of the driveway by Warrior Girl, his back to his attacker, to form his snowball. Then he turned and ran up the driveway toward Papaw, snowball raised high in the air, yelling like a Viking on the attack. Once he reached pointblank range, he fired and hit his target about half the time.

He turned and ran back down the driveway, laughing as soon as the snowball was launched — he didn't even wait to see if he hit his target. Fire and run! Ricochet was methodical in his attack, playing odds and probabilities to his advantage.

While ADHD is a disability, this snowball war showed me it does not debilitate all facets. Individuals with ADHD have talents and gifts, too. Ricochet approached many things in his play strategically, and I recognized right then that would be a blessing in his future.

The first time school let Ricochet down

I pushed open the heavy wood door to the Special Education classroom. In front of me sat three staff members in tiny student chairs around a very short table. I entered, overwhelmed by the thought of a meeting determining my child's Special Education qualification. The sight of those teachers and administrators together gave me an instant us-against-them lump in my throat. The instinct to turn and run surfaced, if only I could have.

A Special Education teacher invited me in. "Come on in and sit down, Mrs. Williams." *Ah, this is going to be formal.*

Ms. Marvelous was there, and the facilitator introduced me to the others involved in the meeting. I sat down and took out a notebook and pen. I had no idea what to expect, but I figured having pen and paper handy was always a safe bet.

They handed me a stack of stapled papers — test scores and reports from their evaluation. She first reviewed Ricochet's test scores with the group, reading them one by one. As the meeting progressed, she grew fidgety and shuffled through the papers awkwardly. We turned to the last page in the reporting, the school psychologist's evaluation and recommendations. I scanned the page quickly and stopped in my tracks when I came to the last line. It read, "Classroom accommodations are ideal for this student. I do not recommend an IEP."

About the time I read that line, she said, "So, Ricochet does not qualify for Special Education services."

How can that be? The educational staff has my child's best interests as priority number one, which is their job. The laws surrounding disabilities in the classroom were designed to help children achieve academic success. These great people acting under these great laws, coupled with the report from Ricochet's developmental specialist and OT, certainly prove that Ricochet needs help in school to achieve his definition of greatness.

My child was struggling immensely in school — how could he not qualify for Special Education? I can't help but feel angry, disappointed, and completely helpless during times like these. How could anyone see how much Ricochet struggled with handwriting and deny him OT?

I put my signature to a lie that day — I signed a document stating that Ricochet's disability did not hinder his academic achievement. He had average or better grades for reading and math, but earned low scores in writing. How was that not affecting his academics? If he didn't have a problem with writing, he would no doubt receive average or better scores in writing, too.

I only requested testing for Special Education for his writing. I knew that 504 Plan accommodations would help to limit the effect of his ADHD on achievement, if implemented properly. It couldn't improve his writing, though.

Ricochet was denied Special Education services simply because he was smart. His Full Scale IQ was "above average" on the intelligence test. He scored very well on the achievement tests as well. In fact, he scored above average in everything except Writing Fluency and Reading Vocabulary.

That was no surprise to me. I knew Ricochet was very bright. Even his kindergarten teacher knew he was very intelligent, and she didn't like to say *anything* nice about him. Ms. Marvelous knew he was super smart, too. After experiencing his behavior and lack of achievement, everyone was shocked to discover how intelligent he really was. That very disconnect led me to look for a learning disability, and it was apparently going to keep him from the extra help he needed, too.

As I drove home from the meeting, my heart was heavy. I planned to begin the process to ensure a 504 Plan for Ricochet. That legal document would spell out appropriate classroom accommodations to even the playing field and the school had to follow it. I really didn't want a 504 Plan though; that was merely a crutch. The 504 accommodations — like verbally spelling words on his test his teacher couldn't read and shorter reading homework — would help him not be penalized for ADHD symptoms, but they wouldn't provide services to work on his deficiencies. Inability to finish assignments and poor scores on timed tests due to inattention were holding him back. Then there were actual deficiencies, like handwriting. The 504 would allow him to use a word processor for assignments instead of writing them by hand to get by, but it didn't provide services to help him improve his handwriting skills so he wouldn't need the word processor.

I had been told that my child is gifted and didn't need Special Education, yet I was sad. I was devastated, and then felt ungrateful and miserable. I knew I couldn't be the first parent saddened when the Special Education department rejected their child, though. There are thousands of children who walk the line between mainstream education and special services, like Ricochet. There are many children whose intelligence overshadows their special needs. It's numbingly ironic.

Time to put on my first pair of boxing gloves

The more I perseverated on the fact that Ricochet was denied Special Education, the angrier I became. This child truly needed extra help, and I couldn't obtain it. Instead, I was to allow them to put a Band-Aid on his school struggles, in the form of a 504 Plan, and sit back and accept that he was struggling and miserable. *Uh, no. Not this momma.*

I couldn't pretend that Ricochet's disability didn't have "an adverse effect on educational performance" as his school could. Intelligence is not a measure of performance, and I was ready to fight to prove it. I swiftly sent the following letter to our School Board's Exceptional Children Director. The letter summed up why I chose to appeal.

Ms. Director,

I'm seeking information on the appeals process for Special Education services. I found your contact information in the front of the *Procedural Safeguards: Handbook on Parent's Rights* I was given by the school.

My son, Ricochet, is a 1st grade student at [our] Elementary. He was diagnosed with ADHD in November, 2008. He was also found to have fine motor skills and handwriting impairment by an Occupational Therapist who evaluated him. The Special Education Department began testing him, at my request, since before his diagnoses.

On Thursday, 3/5/2008, I was invited to a meeting with his IEP team to discuss the results. I was informed that his IQ test placed him at high average and, therefore, he does not need "specially designed instruction." On the eligibility worksheet, it asks, "What is the adverse effect on educational performance?" One of the school representatives answered that question, "At this point, Ricochet's achievement is in the high average range for his age, despite his inattention."

There are two inaccuracies in this answer:

1. His performance should be measured by what he is able to accomplish in the classroom and on his report card, not a test of his intelligence/ capability. I asked for Special Ed because he is very smart but is struggling in the classroom. His fantastic teachers have been able to bring him up to grade level in reading and math now. However, his writing is still below grade level. Despite his intelligence, he cannot perform in this area.

2. Ricochet takes ADHD medication to help control his inattention and focus. I have always understood that accommodations would address these issues, and never expected Special Ed services for these issues. The sole reason I asked that he be evaluated for Special Ed and not just given a 504 was to address his need for Occupational Therapy as it relates to writing — a skill absolutely necessary for school success. There is a 2-page OT report in which she describes Ricochet's difficulty with pencil grip, letter formations, spacing, legibility, etc., and even mentions that he required 1:1 attention to get through the task. She also mentions oral-motor and sensory needs, which absolutely affect classroom performance.

I understand that Ricochet is being referred to the 504 committee and that he will likely qualify for formal accommodations. Accommodations for his ADHD are completely necessary, and he receives some through the attentiveness of his teacher already. However, giving in to the fact that he will be allowed to use a word processor in a later grade does not explore whether or not he can improve his writing skills with special instruction and OT and never need that type of accommodation/crutch. To not try to overcome these deficiencies before resorting to an accommodation to address it is frankly letting down a child who could possibly reach his potential (measured in that IQ test) with extra help.

You now have my viewpoint and understand why I chose to appeal this decision. I am not angry, but I am

going to fight for what my son needs to be successful in school and in his life. Please respond to let me know what steps I need to take to appeal this decision. I copied school administration so they are aware of our correspondence. Thank you in advance for your assistance in this matter.
Kindly,
Penny

I dreaded the appeal process — one of my biggest fears is public speaking, and I was sure to have to speak to a group if I took the school to court! However, I was determined to do whatever it took to ensure my son received the help required to succeed.

I received a quick response to my letter from the Exceptional Children Director outlining the appeal process. She offered to have her staff review the evaluation results and meet with me to reach a resolution. I was happy with her response.

Ricochet had a follow-up with the developmental doctor the following day. I showed him the school evaluation.

"His IQ is fantastic, and his achievement scores are good as well," the doctor said to me. "Why appeal the Special Education denial when Ricochet doesn't need it? He's very smart."

What was with everyone thinking a smart child couldn't possibly need Special Education services?

I responded frankly, "I need the school to provide occupational therapy for him."

"Why don't you just take care of it privately?" he asked. Of course it seemed simple to him; he was living on a doctor's income.

My cheeks felt inflamed. "We can't afford to right now," I answered, embarrassed to have to say that aloud.

"You're not going to get Special Education services for the little bit of OT he needs." It would have been nice to hear a bit of compassion in his voice, but I did not.

"Visiting the OT center here in your practice is billed by the hospital and goes against our deductible. I had to pay $200 for the OT evaluation Ricochet already had here, and there's no way we could pay $200 a week for continued OT. Can you recommend another facility in town then? One not affiliated with the hospital? If we use a facility not affiliated with the hospital, it costs us one quarter of that. We could probably afford that copay a couple of times a month."

"No," he said, curtly. He was done with me and with Ricochet's appointment.

At least he didn't tell me what I wanted to hear to pacify me, I guess. I hoped the Exceptional Children Director would tell me what I wanted to hear though, and soon.

A week later I heard back — the Assistant Director had offered to "deal with me." We spoke about Ricochet, his diagnoses, and his continued classroom struggles. She studied his evaluations, but didn't feel she had enough clarity to make a decision yet. The following week, she personally went to the classroom to observe Ricochet. She called me that afternoon with a decision. She could not approve him for Special Education. *Ugh!*

She explained that Federal Law states that a child must qualify for general Special Education inclusion with one of fourteen disabilities before they can be evaluated for specific special services. Occupational therapy is one of the special services only accessible to one of those specific fourteen disabilities.

- Autistic
- Deaf
- Seriously emotionally disabled
- Deaf-Blind
- Hearing impaired
- Multi-handicapped
- Intellectually disabled
- Orthopedically impaired
- Other health impaired (includes ADD/ADHD)
- Specific learning disabled
- Speech/language disabled
- Traumatic brain injured
- Visually impaired

While ADHD is included in the "other health impaired" category, the federal law also states: "...if it is determined...that a child has one of the disabilities...but only needs a related service and not a special education, the child is not a child with a disability under [the law]."

How do you determine if a child with ADHD needs a special education and not just a related service? When I spoke to the assistant director the last time, I finally felt some clarity on the categories of disabilities. The IEP team determined that Ricochet needed a related service, but not a "special education." I didn't understand how one was so different from the other, or why the law is structured to turn away students who are only a little disabled, those who have only one need. It's still a need.

I decided I was going to accept this woman's final decision because she was working so hard to understand Ricochet and his unique set of circumstances. I felt certain she would be thorough and fair, and that's all I could expect. Once she explained it to me in terms I could actually understand, I felt she was thorough and fair under the law. The outcome wasn't what I expected, nor what I wanted, but I'd rise to fight another day for my sweet son...

I moved on to find out exactly what inclusion in Section 504 meant for my son. I found a memo from Jeanette J. Lim, Acting Assistant Secretary for Civil Rights and the US Department of Ed, on Section 504.[4] It states very specifically that a child qualifying for Section 504 is entitled to special services and cannot be denied because they didn't qualify under IDEA, the law that outlines students' rights to special education. *What?!* That said to me that Ricochet could receive services through a 504 Plan, but I was told that he must qualify for Special Education to receive any services. If he could get some "services" through a 504 Plan and not just accommodations (what I considered workarounds and crutches), then I was all for moving on to 504 Committee. I was pushing hard for Special Education and an IEP because my understanding was that it must be Special Education to get "extra help" and a 504 Plan would only offer accommodations.

The bottom line for Ricochet? Who knew? I sure didn't. I knew the only thing left to do for Special Education was to file a formal due process petition, a court proceeding that would require lots of resources and many months.

I felt like he'd be denied again there for this same "if a child only needs one service, they don't qualify under IDEA" loophole. We moved on to 504 Committee at that point for our sanity and for the sake of Ricochet. The longer I fought for Special Education inclusion, the longer he went without any formal policy to address his specific needs. That didn't benefit him either.

I read everything I could get my hands on about Section 504 law while waiting for the meeting. If I received any push-back on creating a 504 Plan for Ricochet, I would be armed and ready to defend. I hoped the process would be shorter than the months we waited for a decision on Special Education inclusion.

Admitting defeat and moving on

My hands were trembling and my stomach was in my throat as I headed down the school corridor toward the office a couple weeks later. I wasn't intimidated by the group I'd face in this meeting because I already knew most of them. I feared the outcome would not be in Ricochet's favor. I was terrified they'd deny him a 504 Plan or reject the list of appropriate accommodations I had drafted.

I worked diligently for nine months to get a diagnosis for Ricochet and the accommodations he needed for academic success. We had already been denied inclusion in Special Education, so I felt a bit defeated and a lot helpless as I sat down among the 504 committee members. I felt Ricochet truly qualified for Special Education and needed special services. I felt the "system" was against us. I feared that each law to help and protect kids like Ricochet had a gaping crack that he would fall through again.

In attendance were: the assistant principal, who heads the 504 program for this school; Ms. Marvelous; the school's Occupational Therapist; and the 504 Program Coordinator for our Board of Education.

I concentrated all morning on erasing defeat from my face. I organized my documents on Ricochet's testing and diagnosis, his OT evaluations and handwriting samples, and chewed pencils that now looked more like shivs. I copied 504 sample accommodations for ADHD and highlighted those I thought would benefit Ricochet. I went armed with a Q & A from the US Department of Education on Section 504 Law, too. I was prepared for a fight.

Thankfully, a fight was not necessary this time. The first item on the "Section 504/ADA Student Accommodation Plan" form was "eligible" or "not eligible." As the assistant principal completed the form by talking himself through it, he said, "Yes, he is eligible under Section 504," before any conversation could commence. I could breathe again.

We listed Ricochet's major life activities affected by his ADHD:

Learning, concentration, communication, sensory deficit creates needs for excessive movement and oral stimulation, and auditory processing.

I did not expect the list to be so long, but was relieved by the acknowledgment.

How do those impairments impact him in the school environment?

Requires more freedom of movement, and classroom activities require accommodations.

Accommodations in the classroom and for standardized testing were written into Ricochet's 504 Plan as follows:

- Use of chewing gum in the classroom with appropriate restrictions (This had to be approved by the principal and was the following day. Ironic because, the more we talked about Ricochet's chewing problem and the dangers of what he was chewing, everyone in the room thought chewing gum was the best solution.)
- Other appropriate oral-motor tools as needed
- Provide taped area around Ricochet's desk so he can work in the area and still be considered on task without being required to sit still in his chair (Ms. Marvelous was doing that already)
- Preferred seating away from distractions and near the teacher (already implemented)
- Explore use of seating disc to satisfy movement needs (The OT recommended it before I could.)
- Posting of schedule and rules in the classroom (already done). Also post visual reminders of items to pack for take-home each day.
- Transition plan
- Use of visual cue cards for behavior (already implemented as part of Ms. Marvelous's teaching style)
- Positive behavior support (already implemented)
- Custom behavior plan for Ricochet with daily feedback and rewards (already implemented)
- Re-direct as needed (already implemented)

- Provide writing accommodations such as slant board, specialized writing paper, pencil grips, etc.
- Consider "Handwriting Without Tears" program (They would only commit to "considering" this due to restrictive budget.)
- Provide scissors he is comfortable with, reserved for him (I had already sent a pair in.)
- "Heavy" work opportunities, e.g., carrying a stack of books to the library, carrying a basket of outdoor toys to the playground, etc.
- Provide movement opportunities (bathroom, drink of water, take note to office...)
- Allow "fidget" tools
- Allow Ricochet to orally spell words on the written test that the teacher can't read

My only complaint about the meeting and final Accommodation Plan was that the school was very guarded and as vague as possible on the form. They knew anything written there had to be provided by law, so words like "possibly", "look into", "explore", and "consider" were used excessively. They would not commit to anything that required a purchase. I became rather annoyed by the third financial discussion. However, I decided to give them the benefit of the doubt and believe they would implement all recommendations, as necessary, unless they showed otherwise. I was pleased overall and not willing to "stir the pot" at that time.

We were finally solidifying a plan for Ricochet's academic success with only six weeks left in the school year. I wondered how many of the items not already implemented would be before first grade was over. Everything was set for second grade, which was my ultimate goal.

His subsequent teacher would be hand-picked by the principal with these accommodations in mind. He would be placed with a teacher with as similar a teaching style to Ms. Marvelous as possible. Ms. Marvelous even voluntarily met with the new teacher before the next school year started to discuss Ricochet's needs.

Now I felt a little lost. For months, I had spent a ton of time and effort educating myself about ADHD and IDEA and Section 504 laws. I fought for a long time for testing and inclusion and for medication that worked. When things began to level out, I felt like there was something I should have been doing but wasn't, as if I were forgetting something. I knew there would be other obstacles to overcome and battles to fight, so I stored that extra energy for the next round.

Finally seeing Ricochet

At the beginning of first grade, Ricochet had been below grade level in every subject. He could only read a few sight words, couldn't write even his name legibly, and didn't have any real experience with math. By the end of the grade, seven months into his ADHD treatment, he was reading on the level expected, above grade level in math, and willing to try writing at least 60% of the time. He had refused to do any school work before he was diagnosed; it was just too difficult for him. The content of the work wasn't too difficult, except in writing. It was simply too difficult to focus on the work and complete it.

Ms. Marvelous was the best teacher for him, and his being in her class was purely happenstance. She immediately made several accommodations to provide an environment in which he could learn. I'm confident he made some progress just through her classroom accommodations, but medication contributed the greatest difference. Once Ricochet had effective medication, he could slow down and focus enough to use the accommodations and let his smarts shine through.

Before diagnosis, Ricochet was a very sad little boy. He was very aware that he couldn't accomplish what his peers could, and that he couldn't control his behavior enough to please his elders. He was too young to tell us that it wasn't in his control, so he got in an angry huff, and the enormity of the frustration lead to tears. A gut-wrenching, belly cry with big crocodile tears took place almost daily.

Now, at this point in his treatment, he was joyful. He received a lot of praise and loved it. He was full of pride, too. Yes, there were still times when things just didn't go as he wanted, but the change was truly life-altering for our entire family.

I now realized ADHD can be a gift, if you let it be. The challenges ADHD bestows can't be removed, but they can be managed and worked around. I knew there were many tough times down the road, but resolved to take them as they come. Ricochet's intelligence, creativity, and ingenuity were now shining through. That was a great accomplishment for seven months, and I was hopeful for what the next seven months would bring. I expected mostly smooth sailing from then on.

3
Simply Trying to Get Through Each Day

"Your assumptions are your windows on the world. Scrub them off every once in a while, or the light won't come in."
— *Isaac Asimov*

An unexpected change truly can be the end of the world

Warrior Girl joined Girl Scouts while attending the kids' prior charter school, and her troop still met there after the kids left. Every Thursday, I picked up Ricochet and Warrior Girl after school and headed to the "old school" for the Girl Scout meeting.

Ricochet was good friends with the troop leader's son. He had been Ricochet's only good friend the previous year, so of course he had missed him since changing schools. The troop leader and I agreed that the boys would both come to the meetings and have a chance to play together. There were a couple of other little brothers of Girl Scouts, too, so the boys had their own little "meeting." Ricochet *really* looked forward to Thursdays.

This particular Thursday was different from no other. We arrived at the school as usual. Warrior Girl ran in to join the other girls, and Ricochet perched right inside the doorway, scanning the room for his friend.

He immediately asked the leader, "Where is Little M?"

"He went home with his great grandmother, sweetie."

{Strike 1}

The leader turned to me, and said, "You have to leave. The girls are making Mother's Day presents, and they are a surprise. You can't be here next week, either."

I'm afraid I wasn't very polite. "It would have been nice if someone told us these things ahead of time so we could plan for them," I snapped.

She was sure someone had mentioned it, and I was sure I'd heard nothing of the sort — I did not know. Either way, all I could do at that point was brace for the fallout.

I certainly thought making Mother's Day gifts was wonderful, but I knew this sudden change in plan, a plan we had followed consistently for eight months prior, was going to upset Ricochet, and then some.

"Buddy," I said in my sugary Glinda-the-Good-Witch voice, "we have to leave now. They are making a surprise for Mother's Day."

Crying immediately commenced. His sobs echoed down the long hall to the exit. It was reminiscent of his days as a student there, which didn't help. He tried to be a big boy and hold it in, but he didn't have the tools to handle disappointment well.

My sister lived close by, and I knew Creative H and Grandma would be at her house. I suspected seeing his cousin and playing her Wii would distract Ricochet from his disappointment and make everything better.

Playing Wii had Ricochet feeling good for a little while, until he became painfully aware that his younger, female cousin was beating him at every game. Grandma and I tried to explain that she'd had lots of practice, which made her score higher. He didn't want to hear any of that, he wanted to win a game. He insisted, not very kindly, that Creative H go easy on him and be a better sport.

"Creative H is just trying her best, which is what we should all do. She is not being a bad sport, but you are because you are being a sore loser."

After the third or fourth loss, Ricochet began to break down and cry again. He continued to play, but was tormented every time she scored higher than he did, which was most of the time.

{Strike 2}

We made it through the hour, and Ricochet got his shoes right on, very obediently, when it was time to go. *Home free!* As we walked toward the door, he realized he was thirsty. He asked if he could take a drink with him. I knew there were juice boxes in the refrigerator, and offered for him to pick his flavor. He opened the refrigerator and spotted the fancy (read expensive) Kool-Aid coolers. He was adamant he was taking that kind.

"We should not take the special drinks without asking Auntie or Uncle M, and they are not home," I explained.

His whole little being fell to the floor with a solid thud. With the refrigerator door still open above him, Ricochet cried, yelled at me, and punched me in the shins with all the force he could assemble behind his tiny fists. Each wallop was more than a physical attack, it was a blow to my spirit as well.

{Strike 3.}

I'm out!

I'm afraid I was not very nice once again. I snapped at him, "It is never okay to hit me or anyone else. Get up and take a juice box so we can pick up your sister. We will not worry her by being late." It took an additional ten minutes to get him out the door.

He yelled, "I hate you!" at me all the way to the car. I swear I heard it echo off the mountain faces around us.

Once in the car, Ricochet said, "I'll never love you again," with a calm callousness that struck deep.

By then I was too angry to let his words truly penetrate. I had learned long before that he didn't mean the ugly words he spewed at me in the middle of a meltdown. And, predictably, fifteen minutes later, he was professing his love and trying to smooth things over.

I knew he was thrown for a loop by the change in schedule because he didn't handle sudden changes well at all. I had empathy for the rotten situation. However, I could not allow him to think it's okay to throw a fit, or to hit me or others. I knew his actions were mostly out of his control, but I still had to provide the lesson so he could learn to check himself before it got that far.

I got the same reaction an hour later when I asked him to do his homework.

"The book she gave me to read today is too long," he shouted. "I'm not going to read it. You can't make me read it!"

When I insisted he do it, he yelled, spewing hatred, and punched me again. I sent him to his room so we could both calm down. Once in his room he realized the error of his ways, and cried out, "Momma! Moooommaaaa! Pleeeeeease, Momma!" blubbering the whole time. I was sure not to show forgiveness too quickly that time, though. Sometimes, the only way to learn self-control is for the repercussions to sting a bit. After a few minutes, I let him sit with me, opening my arms as an invitation to cuddle. I held him for quite a while that night.

He never did his homework, and I was fine with that.

I learned a lot that day, though — we could not be flexible when it comes to Ricochet. As much as we might want to, we just could not. He needed warning to transition. I felt sorry if that would be an inconvenience to others, but a change in schedule was much more than an inconvenience for Ricochet.

Determination, a blessing and a curse

One day that spring, I allowed the kids to come outside and play in the driveway while I planted some herbs behind the house. Remember, we lived on a mountain. We had a momma black bear who frequented our house with her new cubs during the warm months every year — it was not always safe for the kids to run outside to play whenever they felt like it. They were both ecstatic to be able to play outside, especially Ricochet.

Warrior Girl was a top-notch tattle-tale at the time, so I was aware that Ricochet had his bike out in the lower part of the driveway. I was fine with that because there was a small, sort-of-level area to circle, and he couldn't go over the edge in that spot. Mr. T and I told both of them a hundred times after purchasing bikes that it was crazy dangerous to ride them at our house due to the steep terrain.

I went about my business planting. A few minutes later, Warrior Girl came around to tell me they were going to walk over to visit Papaw, who was outside working on his house. No problem.

Next thing I knew, I heard a loud banging and realized Mr. T was banging violently on the window overlooking the driveway. He knocked on the window often when they were going too far from the house. I was on my knees, bent over digging a giant hole for my fern and figured he had it under control. Then I heard him banging again, and again. I got up and opened the door and yelled inside to him that I told them it was okay to go over to see Papaw.

"Ricochet just tried to ride his bike down the road and he went over the side!" he yelled in a panic.

My entire body felt flushed. I dropped my shovel and ran as fast as I could out the driveway and down the road to him. Sure enough he had tried to ride his bike down the steep, twenty-degree incline of loose gravel, but had fallen on the road, not over the side of the mountain thankfully. He was standing up next to the bike by the time I got there, crying so hard I couldn't understand what he was saying. I looked him over — no scrapes, no blood. I knew he felt pain, but he wasn't seriously hurt.

"You can go on over to see Papaw if you want," I told him gently.

He picked up his bike and flung his leg over to get back on!

"Whoa, Buddy! You just crashed on your bike big-time trying to ride down this giant hill! Why do you want to do that again?"

"I want to ride my bike," he explained.

"You can't ride your bike here. Didn't you learn that when you fell? You said it hurt, so why would you do it again?"

"I can do it this time!"

"No, sweetie, you can't. This is not a place for bike riding. We'll go talk to Daddy about taking our bikes to the park tomorrow so you can ride, but you can't ride here."

"Yes, I can," he retorted. "I can do it. I'm a big kid."

"You *are* a big kid," I agreed. "But even the best stunt biker probably wouldn't attempt riding down this hill."

"I'm tough, Momma. I can do it."

It took at least ten minutes of trying to reason with him before I could get him to *walk* the bike back home. I finally convinced him by telling him he could ride it in the somewhat-flat area of our driveway again. When we got over there and I watched him try to ride there, I realized it wasn't so flat after all and he couldn't really ride there either. No riding at home. He was, of course, devastated. It was, of course, the end of the world.

I finally offered to take him and his bike down to the park when I was done planting. He was so determined to ride his bike that day that nothing short of an ambulance ride was going to stop him. I couldn't allow that.

There's no stopping that train

When Ricochet sets his mind to something, there's no turning back. When he decided he would ride his bike, go immediately to his cousin's house to play, or go to Lego Club even though it was the wrong day, he would resort to whatever he thought necessary to make it happen. He made demands, shook his little fist at me, and even told me hurtful things like, "I will never love you again." Mind you, this was not his personality at all. When he became fixated on something, there was no stopping that train.

I discovered a great children's play place with a coffee bar and wireless Internet for grownups. While you could go in anytime to play, the owner focused on something specific for an hour or two each day to bring kids with similar interests together. Ricochet's peak interest was the Lego Club she hosted Tuesday afternoons. The very week after I discovered the cafe, I took Ricochet to the Lego playtime before his t-ball game and he had a great time.

The following Monday, the kids were putting on uniforms because they both had ball games.

"Can we go to Lego Club on the way, Momma?" he asked sweetly.

"No, Buddy. It's Monday, and Lego Club is on Tuesdays."

"But she told us she can get out the Legos anytime."

"Yes, that's true. But your ball game starts in less than an hour. We have to get to the field. She will be closing the café by the time we could drive over there. Playing Legos at the café just isn't possible today."

Ricochet opened negotiations. "I will not put my uniform on unless you say you will take me to the café on the way." He crossed his arms tightly over his chest and used his best mean voice.

I asked him a couple of times very politely to get his uniform on so he and his sister weren't late for their games. Polite wasn't working, so I began the count.

"Three...Two...O — "

"I'm putting on my ball clothes!" he squeaked in at the very last second. "But I'm not playing in my game unless you take me to Lego Club first."

I know this sounds like plain ole defiance and stubbornness, but in his neurologically-different mind, Lego Club always happens before a ball game; they were linked for him like peanut butter and jelly. He could not, or maybe would not, accept that it was the wrong day and time.

"I don't care if you play ball tonight or not, but your sister also has a game, and you are going to the ball field now." I was trying to keep my cool, but I was definitely raising my voice by this point. I was thinking, *Son of a B!#@h! Dammit already! Enough! I am the parent here!*

After his refusal to come downstairs, put on his cleats, and carry his water bottle, and reminding me every three seconds that he was not going to play, we made it out the door. Warrior Girl was so upset that he was not going to play in his game that she gave herself a stomachache.

Despite much reverse psychology on the twenty-minute drive to the ball fields, Ricochet was not going to play. I had him go to his coach and tell him in person that he was not playing. I thought he wouldn't have the nerve and decide to just play, but I was wrong. He walked right up and told Coach he didn't want to play. And that was that.

Ricochet had to sit in the girls' dugout with me during Warrior Girl's entire softball game since I was dugout mom and Mr. T was coaching. He sat perfectly still and quiet throughout the entire two hours. I was stunned. About halfway through, I decided he must not be feeling well because those are the only conditions under which he sits still and quiet for that length of time. Reflecting on it later, I concluded that he was really hurt that using everything in his arsenal didn't work.

Naturally, I took him to Lego Club the very next day. His life was hard — I didn't need to make it any harder.

But my son doesn't have high blood pressure

We were back at the developmental doctor for another medication checkup for Ricochet's ADHD treatment. At the last checkup, his doctor had reluctantly increased the dosage of Medication #3, despite concerns about the fact that he had lost five pounds since starting ADHD medication. I was a ball of nerves, biting my nails for days leading up to the appointment. I knew the doctor would change his medication again if Ricochet had lost any more weight. I agreed that he had to grow, but I was also nervous because both his teacher and I had begun to realize Medication #3 was losing effectiveness again (the reason for the increased dose the last time). I don't approach the unknown very willingly.

The nurse weighed and measured him and took his blood pressure to commence the long wait for his doctor. I saw his weight and height, but couldn't remember his stats from the previous checkup, so I was still on the edge of my seat when the doctor finally arrived. He looked at Ricochet's weight first, and shared that it was exactly the same as it had been two months before, down to the tenth of a pound. He was no longer losing weight, which was great news. He grew one and a half inches since diagnosis, too, so the concern that the medication would stunt his growth was diminished.

"Medication #3 is losing effectiveness again. His teacher and I both see it," I said.

"We can't keep increasing the medication," he replied. "You have to accept that this may be as good as it gets."

Hesitantly, I challenged him. "When his medication was working, he did really great. Knowing his potential to do well, how do we accept this and not strive to retain that?"

He answered my challenge with the idea of adding a second daily medication. He told me about a hypertension medication often prescribed to individuals with ADHD when stimulants aren't effective. It was not yet FDA-approved for children and for treating ADHD, but that was slated for later that year.

I didn't like the idea of giving Ricochet two medications every day, nor giving him a medication for high blood pressure when his blood pressure was normal. His doctor explained that it helped with hyperactivity and impulsivity, the two ADHD symptoms Ricochet was again struggling with. He said we could try it for a few days to see if he could take it without severe side effects and if it would help with the re-emerging symptoms.

I filled the prescription and waited for the weekend. I was not okay with giving him a new medication and sending him to school. He started a few days later, despite having a grueling schedule all weekend.

I gave Ricochet a half tablet of the new medication plus his current dose of Medication #3 at about 7:30 AM Saturday morning. By 8:45 AM, I noticed he was much more still and quiet. We left for the Little League field at 9:15 AM. It wasn't five minutes before he was asleep in the backseat. He had not fallen asleep in the car in two or three years, so I was concerned.

I couldn't reach him to check on him, so I asked Warrior Girl to put her hand under his nose and make sure he was still breathing, despite knowing the request would likely freak her out. She calmly did so and reported that he was breathing. I felt like I was over-reacting, but I had just given a child with no heart condition a blood pressure medication he'd never taken before, and he had fallen asleep in the car for the first time in at least two years, within two hours of taking it. Freaking out felt justified.

Ricochet woke up within fifteen minutes, even before we reached our destination — as if he hadn't been asleep. All was well through his game. We then stopped for lunch before Warrior Girl's softball game across town. He didn't complain about not feeling hungry, but it was all I could do to get him to eat five or six Cheetos, which was unusual. His appetite was less than on Medication #3 alone, despite the doctor's assurance otherwise.

Ricochet sat with Grandma, Papaw, Auntie, Uncle M, and Creative H just outside the dugout for the softball game. He came around to the door of the dugout, crying for me, at 2:30 PM. He couldn't be with me in the dugout because it wasn't our home field, so I stood outside the dugout and held him for a bit. He was desperate to be with me, which sometimes happened before the added medication. I gave Grandma the few dollars I had in my pocket, and asked her to take him to the concession stand as a diversion.

Lots of the smaller brothers and sisters of our teammates were wading in a tiny creek beside the field, and during the entire game Ricochet had been begging to do it, too. Grandma finally came to me and asked if he could wade if she stayed with him. "Go for it!" I said. By that time I was losing my sanity with his neediness, and I didn't want to deprive him of such simple childhood pleasures. He, Creative H, and the other six little sprites had a great time walking back and forth in the creek.

On our way home, Ricochet fell asleep again after just a few minutes in the car. Warrior Girl again checked to see if he was breathing. I didn't ask her to, but I took the opportunity to remind her that she knows she loves him in those moments.

Sunday morning, I gave Ricochet his medications again, and we headed for the local baseball game at about 1 PM. It was raining and cold, miserable for a baseball game, but we already had the kids' tickets for that game, and the rain was supposed to clear out.

We sat on the bleachers for two hours, watching them pull the tarp off the field, then put it right back on. We had a snack to try to pass the time, but Ricochet was bored and whiny. He sat very still and laid his head on my arm nearly the entire time. Before medications, he would have been bouncing all over the place, up and down the risers, and in trouble. They finally called the game, and we went home. He didn't fall asleep at odd times that day, and he ate a good dinner.

On the third day of the new, additional medication, Ricochet's teacher said he didn't eat much lunch, but was considerably less impulsive. She said he was humming and singing a lot, but the medicine seemed to be helping. I planned a conference in the next week or two to find out if the combination of medications was covering all symptoms in first grade now.

The proverbial fine line

In our family there's a fine line between fun, happy family time and a car ride home early with at least two of us in tears (three out of four in tears this particular spring Sunday). The line is so fine there's just no straddling it. We tended to hover close, then fall head-first right over the line. That's our reality with the unpredictability of ADHD.

Warrior Girl was very into softball, and Ricochet enjoyed the outdoor aspect of being on a t-ball team. That year, we joined the Kid's Club of our local AAA Baseball Team, which provided super-cheap kid tickets to every Sunday game. In years past, it was difficult to take Ricochet to the ball game because he couldn't sit still for a moment, much less three hours. Now that his ADHD was being treated, he enjoyed the games a little. Though we couldn't get through one Sunday ball game without an ADHD-induced crisis, typically over food.

"I want a snow cone," Ricochet said innocently. "Come on, Momma."

"You already had a hot dog, popcorn, and a big soda," I explained to him, certain that's all he needed.

"But now I want a snow cone," he whined.

"I can't afford to buy you anything else to eat right now."

"But I want a snow cone," he whined again, this time slamming his foot on the ground. Tears welled up in his eyes.

"I just can't do it, baby," I explained with empathy for his situation. "The food is expensive here, and I just can't buy everything you want."

"I want a snow cone," he sobbed.

And so it went. He was then hyper-focused on the snow cone, and everyone was miserable for at least thirty minutes. Warrior Girl wanted it to stop, Mr. T wanted to leave to avoid an embarrassing scene, and I simply wanted everyone to be happy. I'm not sure how we got out of such deep muck.

This day, there was a whole new problem. The park staff inflated two beach balls and sent them up into the stadium for the crowd to smack around. At first, I thought it was a great idea, and I knew the kids would love it. But, like so many other things, it quickly turned south. Ricochet was desperate to hit the ball, but every time it came our way, the boy in front of us would jump up, a good foot higher than Ricochet, and hit the ball in another direction.

Every. Single. Time.

Ricochet cried because he wasn't getting a turn, the kid in front of us was a jack-in-the-box, and I had to watch the dang beach balls to be sure I wasn't going to get one in the head. Two innings later, I was so mad that it was ruining the game for us that I wanted to move out of the middle of the stadium. Ricochet finally got to hit it once and was satisfied, so we got up and looked for enough room in the shade for all four of us. The stadium was more packed than I'd ever seen, and the only open seats were in the sun. Now Mr. T was angry with me for making us move, even though he validated my complaint, and begrudgingly said we'd just have to sit in the sun.

We parked our behinds on very hot metal bleachers in the full late-May sun. Ricochet felt he couldn't handle the heat, and the drunk next to us made fun of the names of each visiting batter as loudly and childishly as he could. Ricochet was melting, Warrior Girl was scared of the mean drunk, and I was approaching my own meltdown.

"Hun, we need to move again," I said with all the gentleness I could muster. "It's too hot here, and being near this drunk is scaring the kids."

"What!" Now Mr. T was also thoroughly pissed. "We just need to go home," he snarled.

"No, I don't want to leave. I want to watch the game, but not right here. Warrior Girl wants to watch the game, too. We can't punish her because of all this other nonsense going on around us." I wasn't whining, but pleading, I'm sure.

As soon as Ricochet heard a suggestion to go home, there was no going back. "Yeah, let's go home. I want to go home. Come on, let's go!"

As we discussed the idea of trying to find one last place to sit and finish out the game, he spiraled. He hyper-focused and had an all-out meltdown on the concrete floor of the concourse as we were leaving. At least we were in the shade.

I tried to reason with Ricochet, "Everyone wants to watch more of the ballgame, and the kind thing to do would be to stay a little longer."

He couldn't decide which way to go once I brought kindness into it. He wanted so badly to be kind, but he couldn't overcome the thought of getting into the car with his beloved Blankie to soothe him and going home.

We fell over that very fine line between normalcy and ADHD-induced hell. So go home we did.

As we drove away from the stadium mid-game, Mr. T and I talked about how sometimes in our world, things were not going to turn out as we expected, no matter how hard we tried. Sometimes we were going to pay for admission and expensive drinks and snacks and only get to enjoy part of the experience. Sometimes it would be a rip-off and wouldn't be fair to everyone, and that's the way it was for our family. I was sad for Warrior Girl — she didn't want to go home, she didn't deserve to get snapped at when we were frustrated, and she shouldn't be punished when we must accommodate for ADHD.

I must not have heard that right

A fairly uneventful week later, Ricochet asked me if he and I could do some homework together as soon as we got home from school. I thought I must have misheard him.

"Did you say you want to do *homework?*" I asked.

"Yes! Homework!" he answered with glee.

"Today was the last day of school. There's no homework, Buddy."

"Ms. Marvelous gave me a math workbook to do over the summer," he explained. "And I want to try the new pencil grips you bought me."

My smile stretched from ear to ear. When Ricochet felt confident, he wanted to do things that were typically hard for him. My little boy with at least two pervasive learning disabilities *asked* to do homework, even when there wasn't any homework to be done. Hallelujah!

Warrior Girl immediately jumped in, "I'm *not* doing any homework!"

Of course not, I thought.

Despite being elated by Ricochet asking to do homework when there wasn't any, it was a sad day in our family, too. It was his last day as a student of Ms. Marvelous. She forever changed the course of his life for the better. She was calm, kind, compassionate, caring, open-minded, open-hearted, genuine, selfless, even-tempered... I could go on all day. She was the best teacher I had ever encountered. She was aware of each child's learning style and individual needs. She was one of a new age of teachers who understand and celebrate the need for movement and, most importantly, individuality.

During the last six weeks of that school year, I teared up every time I thought of Ricochet at school but not in her classroom. I was going to miss my confidant, the one other person who truly understood Ricochet's struggles *and* his wonderfulness, the one other person who worked so hard every day to help him reach his potential. What was so amazing though, was that she put that much time, heart, and soul into every one of her twenty-three students — they were all equally needing and deserving in her eyes.

Acknowledgment without giving power

That summer after first grade I worked toward predictability for Ricochet. That goal was much harder than I anticipated. Things happen. Clients come into town, hairdressers get sick, the weather is unseasonably hot... Ricochet accepted these sudden changes in plan with very little trauma. Maybe he acclimated to summer, instead of me trying to acclimate summer to him. I was certainly open to that.

He was doing remarkably well, actually. I filled and posted a weekly dry-erase calendar each Monday. We also discussed our day most mornings. I tried to set realistic expectations to reduce disappointment.

We were discussing the weekend plan when my words bit me.

"We have ball practice Saturday morning," I said.

Ricochet snapped his head around. "I have ball practice? I thought ball was over."

Oops.

That little word "we" instead of specifying "Warrior Girl" opened a huge can of worms.

"Practice is starting for Warrior Girl's All-Stars team," I explained. "Your t-ball season *is* over."

I quickly held my breath. For the first time in three years of t-ball, he asked why he was not on the All-Stars team like his sister always was.

My face felt flushed. My heart began to pound. I was panicking. I didn't know how to explain to my sweet little guy why he was not on the All Stars team without focusing on his disability. I didn't want to give that power to his ADHD. I believed he was different, not disabled. How did I explain that he wasn't chosen for the All-Stars team because his ADHD made it impossible for him to focus on the game and be a "valuable" player? How would I explain that he was different without the negativity?

I'll tell you how I did it, I side-stepped and avoided the question altogether. I know, "Way to let ADHD have the power anyway." I hear you, and that's 100% right. Warrior Girl butted right in, trying to help, but I changed the topic of conversation in a jiffy, afraid she might make him feel bad while intending to make him feel better.

I continued to kid myself, believing that ADHD wasn't a disability. The problem was that the world wasn't organized for those with differences, it was organized purely for the conformers. We worked extra hard to help Ricochet create systems and an environment that was friendly to his way of bumping around in this world.

But I started to realize I could not always remove the disability and make it okay.

4
Settling In

"Be who you are and say what you feel, because those who mind
don't matter and those who matter don't mind."
— Dr. Seuss

His path to my heart

Our family was hanging out at home one Friday night
the weekend before Father's Day, all doing our separate
things, just before the kids' bedtime. Warrior Girl was on
the Internet, I was blogging on the computer, and Daddy
was roaming around doing different things, all typical.
Ricochet was not building Legos as usual, though.
He was writing. Yep, that's right, he was writing — a
nemesis task he fought hard to avoid on a daily basis. I
was intrigued.

Ricochet loved to fill the walls with whatever he was
fixated on at that moment. Ironically, it was almost always
notes he had written himself. This time, he was making a
path, a trail of breadcrumbs of sorts. One path was mapped
for me, and one for Mr. T. He clung to my shadow as

I followed the arrows on the dozens of Post-its marked with green; those were Momma's Post-its. When I got to his closet door, the Post-it read "bingo." Then I looked in the closet and saw the most beautiful note. It read, "I love you, Mom." It was written clear as day. No interpretation needed as was usually the case with his illegible writing.

Then it was Mr. T's turn, and my heart melted. I was the one who spent the most face time with Ricochet since my business was so slow and Mr. T was at work, so he often forgot to include his daddy in these things. I was so pleased he made Mr. T his very own trail of Post-its. Mr. T was proud and gushy, just like me.

Ricochet gave us both the best parent gift, the enormous gift of showing his love for us and showing us he will be okay. He is such a blessing, ADHD and all.

ADHD + overtired = disaster

We had a long couple of weeks in late June that summer. While we were thrilled that Warrior Girl was invited to play on the All-Stars softball team, it meant several very late nights and a lot of pressure and stress on everyone. One of those weeks alone, between softball games and Independence Day fireworks, we were out until 11 PM or later at least four nights. Ricochet and Warrior Girl usually hit the sheets by eight every night, so that was super late for them.

Ricochet loved to go to the ball field, even when he was not playing, because there were a lot of little brothers for him to play with. I tried to talk him into staying with Grandma and Papaw for the late games, but he wouldn't hear of it. I had to manage him, in public, for several hours after his medicine had worn off. By then, he was totally impulsive, into everything, and didn't play as well with others — there were many more arguments with friends I had to dissolve at that time of night. All this while I tried to watch Warrior Girl play and keep the score book for her games.

I was thrilled when Ricochet finally agreed to spend the night with Grandma and Papaw after not getting home until midnight the night before. He had a very hard time being left out of anything Warrior Girl, Mr. T, and I did, so I was shocked when he agreed. But I really played it up. I told him how they'd play games with him, and Grandma would let him stay up a little past bedtime.

Exhaustion kicked in, and Ricochet had a meltdown early that afternoon. I asked him to pick up his room before swimming lessons and his sleepover. He went up right away, but came back crying after a few minutes. He had dumped the three big buckets that contained all of his toys the day before. When he arrived in his bedroom with the task of cleaning up, he was immediately overwhelmed and decided he needed help. My rule was, if you can take it out, you can clean it up. I didn't clean up their rooms after them.

Grandma and Creative H were there and offered to help him. But Creative H had been getting under his skin earlier that day, and he didn't want her in his room. That was a sorry time to decide to turn someone away — she would have practically cleaned it all up for him.

He was hyper-focused now, and there was no stopping this runaway train. He sat on his bed, arms crossed, brow furled, lips so pursed they stuck straight out, a complete scowl. It was his way or no way, and he thought he was going to enforce that.

Time was limited, and I had no more time to argue with him. Grandma and Creative H left his room since he refused their help. I jumped in the shower, despite Ricochet screaming, throwing things, and promising me that he wasn't cleaning his room and he wasn't going to lose any privileges either. I suggested he curl up in my bed with his Blankie and calm himself down. He refused, so I decided to ignore him. Telling him over and over how it was and how it was going to be was only adding fuel to the fire. He knew what he had to do and what the consequences would be. He came in the bathroom, punched the shower curtain repeatedly, and yelled when I didn't answer his demands. He was so angry that I wasn't answering him, I thought he was going to pull the shower curtain to the floor.

After he screamed, "Do you hear me, Mom?" as loudly as he could eight or nine times, all was suddenly quiet. Hallelujah! The meltdown had ended. I finished my shower and went out to check on him. I assumed he had decided to clean his room, but I actually found him sleeping in my bed. He was so tired from all our late nights and hectic schedule that he was able to go to sleep, even on stimulants, which never happened. I knew by then to never wake a sleeping child, especially if that child has ADHD.

I went into his room, closed the door, and cleaned up his toys. I told myself nothing was worth all the anger and disappointment. I knew the magnitude of the cleanup was just too overwhelming for a kid with the disorganized mind of ADHD. There was always another day to teach him he must put away what he took out.

He woke up shortly after I finished cleaning his room and was back to his sweet self. He discovered his tidy bedroom and thanked me over and over. I looked him in the eye and told him very matter-of-factly that I would not be the one to clean up his room again, no matter how big the mess, and he assured me I'd never have to.

We went downstairs to find Creative H and Grandma. Fortunately, Grandma had not thought better of having him over for the night. She knew those things happened with her grandson sometimes, and I think it made her want to love on him even more. They had a great time together that night, and I was able to enjoy one of Warrior Girl's softball games without worrying about Ricochet's late-night behavior. There was peace after such a fierce storm.

Do I even have to say it? Here we go again.

By now, I couldn't possibly count how many different medications, combinations, and dosages Ricochet had tried to treat his ADHD. It had been eight months since his diagnosis, and we were still making adjustments, trying to find the concoction that worked best for his unique constellation of ADHD symptoms.

He had another checkup with the developmental specialist. I always dreaded these appointments.

"Ricochet's medication seems patchy the last couple weeks," I explained to the doctor. "Sometimes it's perfect and other times, often right in the middle of the day at peak medication, it's as if he hasn't taken a thing. He's even more hyper and less attentive than he was without medication at times."

"The FDA has now approved his secondary medication for treating ADHD in children. Ricochet is only taking half of the smallest dose they tested in the clinical trials to get this approval." He paused, waiting for my I-don't-want-to-give-my-child-more-medicine reaction. I was silent. "We should increase this medication to a full milligram tablet twice a day," he continued. "I think this will help in conjunction with the stimulant he takes."

I wasn't thrilled about the increase. Frankly, I didn't like giving him medication for what seemed like just a behavioral problem in the first place, especially not blood pressure medication. The guilt for turning to medication to treat Ricochet's ADHD was already overwhelming, and every increase in dosage jacked it up higher.

I followed the doctor's orders, and the increase in the second medication seemed to work right away. Before the increase, Ricochet was erratic and overly mischievous in the mornings before I came downstairs to prepare breakfast. He made a king-sized mess that took me thirty minutes each morning to clean up since it was far too overwhelming for him to be able to tackle. That stopped with this increase.

My medication anxiety still festered. I figured it always would, but I knew medication was necessary for my little boy's happiness. I'd do whatever I needed to in order to maintain that.

Warm, sweet, and tangy

Ricochet and I had a Saturday afternoon to ourselves that summer, a rare treat. Mr. T was working in his shop, and Warrior Girl was on a spontaneous trip to the movies with a friend.

I could sit on the computer all day and night between blogging about and researching ADHD — there weren't nearly enough hours in the day for all I wanted to accomplish. However, I was determined to spend this time with Ricochet. He was excited to help me bake something with the blueberries I had bought. We sat together and browsed through lots of blueberry recipes on the Internet, and we settled on a coffee cake.

I knew cooking was educational for children, but the kids didn't cook with me much because it was harder to get them to eat foods when they saw every ingredient going in. Boy, was I missing out! Ricochet and I had a blast baking together. He helped with everything from rinsing the blueberries to checking the final product for doneness with a toothpick. He was focused the whole time, partly because his sister wasn't there to fight over who was going to do each task, but also because he felt accomplished and was looking forward to eating his creation in the end. It didn't hurt that I kept saying, "Thanks for letting *me* help *you* bake this," either.

We were off and running. Ricochet read the recipe, reinforcing that he could read, despite his constant insistence that he still couldn't. He measured the ingredients, stirred, sprinkled the cinnamon sugar on top, and watched it bake in the oven. He was completely engaged throughout the entire process, proving that even a child with ADHD can pay attention and follow through in a hands-on project.

His coffee cake was delicious! It was warm, sweet, and tangy — just like an afternoon with my son!

My heart aches differently for my son

It was nearly midnight and darkness had enveloped our home. I was lying in bed watching television and winding down to go to sleep, as I did every night. Just like every other night, and just as much a part of this routine, my heart ached for Ricochet. I wanted so much to climb into his bed and hold him tight all night. He was certainly not a baby anymore, but I felt the need to be his shield and protector, nonetheless.

I didn't have the same aching for Warrior Girl, though, and I felt a sharp pang of guilt about that. She certainly had her own obstacles and challenges too, but somehow I didn't feel like she needed me, right there over her, as much as Ricochet did. Maybe it was because I saw him sad and down so often, or because I saw her being so strong. Maybe it was because she was older or because he was younger, the baby. I love her and wanted to protect her just as much as Ricochet, but I didn't lie in bed at night and ache to hold her. My motherly protection certainly kicked in on her behalf as it should on other occasions, such as every time some tween snot hurt her feelings.

Each night, when all was still and quiet, I ached for Ricochet. I knew it was an ADHD, differently-abled, I'm-his-mom-and-I-can't-fix-it thing. Rationally, I knew he would be okay — he'd find his groove and be successful through his gifts — but I still ached for him and wanted to protect and shield him from the challenges inhibiting his path. I wanted to hold him in the stillness when the obstacles were far from sight. I ached to make it better.

ADHD can defy your expectations

We went camping in a State Park on a little island off the coast of South Carolina in August 2009. I had expected some misery in the Low Country in August — the temperatures would be soaring, and the mosquitoes would swarm. Other than that, I had no idea what to expect on many levels, and that made me anxious. I attempted to pack for every contingency, but our repeated excursions to Wal-Mart that week suggested failure on that front.

The mini-vacation was great fun and a total disaster all rolled into three short days.

We drove through severe thunderstorms to reach the campground. We erected our tent in the deafening darkness and those same heavy downpours. We awoke the first morning to the same storms and water beginning to penetrate our tent. I immediately worried we might have to give up and go home before we really got started.

We had come all that way to see the ocean though and, by golly, we would do it, even in the rain, before considering going back home so soon. The lightning had stopped, so we strolled aimlessly along the beach for quite some time. We had the beach all to ourselves since it was raining, and low tide meant there were many extra things to explore. We found two sand dollars, saw lots of crabs scurrying about among the fallen trees, and played in the rain a bit. By the time we finished our walk, the rain had stopped and the sun was beginning to emerge from the clouds.

Ricochet had a blast boogie boarding in the ocean surf with Mr. T and Warrior Girl. The first time he fell off the board, went under water, and had eyes full of salt water, he yelled and cried. Knowing his fear of going under, I expected him to quit, but the tears lasted about five seconds, and he went right back into the water to do it again... and again... and again. Sometimes, fearlessness comes in handy and fun trumps discomfort.

A child with ADHD isn't always fearless, though. While Ricochet didn't give a second thought to boogie boarding, even though he knew he'd fall in and go under water every time, he was afraid to climb the stairs at the island's lighthouse. I had a feeling he wouldn't go up, so I tried to talk him out of it before we bought tickets.

"Buddy, I know you want to climb the lighthouse, but you can see all the way to the bottom and sometimes that really scares you," I reasoned.

"I don't care," he rebutted.

"But I don't want to buy you a ticket, and then waste the money when you get scared."

"I won't get scared!" He was so excited his physicality was flailing about.

{Sigh} I know how this is going to go.

We climbed one or two flights of stairs, and his body tensed, his face drooped in despair, and his fists clenched the railing, turning his knuckles a ghostly white. He wanted to quit.

"You can do it," Mr. T called down to him. "Don't be scared."

They were very scary stairs, no doubt. They were constructed of thick steel, but the treads were like Swiss cheese so you could see all the way to the bottom as you watched where you stepped. With Mr. T's encouragement, Ricochet proceeded, but more cautiously. He held the railing tightly and moved more slowly.

penny williams

I ended up nearly having a full-blown panic attack myself by the time I got halfway up. At that point, Ricochet had fully conquered his fear and was running ahead and cheering me on.

I looked up to see his bright smile peering over the rail at me. "You can do it, Momma! Come on! Don't be scared."

I was proud of him for sticking with it and making it to the lookout at the top. Warrior Girl was my more anxious child and had no problems with it. I, on the other hand, now know my limitations and will not be climbing another lighthouse.

Ricochet and Warrior Girl had wanted to try fishing for quite some time. There wasn't much opportunity to fish at home, and we didn't even own poles. I suspected neither had the patience required for it, but I discovered there was a pier on the island where you could borrow poles, so I planned to finally take my kiddos fishing. I figured they'd work at it for twenty to thirty minutes before giving up.

It turned out that determination could overcome a lack of attention and patience. We actually fished for a couple of hours. Despite being bored and not catching anything, Ricochet sat on the pier bench, held his pole over the edge, and waited. He honestly just waited, sitting as still and as quiet as I'd ever seen him. I then became concerned that his determination to catch a fish would keep us sitting on that pier all day. Thankfully, he was willing to admit defeat that day and move on.

I had not been brave enough to leave the electronics at home entirely. Each child was allowed to bring one to play during the five-hour road trip. While it would have been no shock if they had begged me to bend that rule, they did not. Outside of the car, they only played electronics for a few minutes around the campfire one night while waiting (forever) for dinner to cook. There were so many more exciting things to do with the beach just a three-minute walk from our tent door that it was never an issue. Nary was a word uttered about TV, either.

Hyper-focus has its place. A beach covered in millions of tiny pieces of sea shells is not one of those places, by the way.

Ricochet was the first to go to sleep every night, despite noisy neighbors and gangs of raccoons that pillaged our campsite once we were tucked still and quiet inside our tent.

Camping was trial and error, just like life. One must make mistakes to reach the really good part. That was a timely reminder.

No doubt we had a lot of problems camping that week. The mosquitoes were horrendous, sending all of us home practically looking like we had the chicken pox. We ran out of clean, dry clothes because we were rained on so often. The raccoons were a nuisance. Low Country in August is tremendously humid... Then I awoke comfortably in my own bed and downloaded my photos from our trip and was all smiles. We collected some great family memories, reinforcing that all the bad will fade away with so much goodness.

The camping excursion was enlightening as well. I realized that ADHD is not such a problem with frequent opportunity for movement and exploration. Ricochet was a perfect gentleman that entire weekend with zero meltdowns. He was content and entertained, wild and free. If only I could provide a life full of these sorts of opportunities, but, the truth is life's not a beach.

Ricochet's first love letter

The morning before the first day of second grade, we attended the Meet the Teacher event at our elementary school. It was an opportunity to see the kids' classrooms and meet their new teachers, although I had met with Ricochet's teacher regarding his special needs once prior.

Ricochet was paradoxically bashful that morning. He hid behind me most of the morning, only peeking out from my waist when his curiosity got the best of him. He was unsure of this new year and classroom, as was I.

We explored as a family, visiting Ricochet's classroom first. I encouraged him to check it out and look around, but he wouldn't budge from the safety of my shadow. His teacher introduced herself, and we completed our paperwork and moved on to Warrior Girl's class.

Mr. T swiftly left for work after meeting her teacher. Warrior Girl was inquisitive and took time to ask lots of questions. But in Warrior Girl's classroom Ricochet remained huddled behind me.

When we were finished in the fifth grade hall, I asked Ricochet if he'd like to go say "Hi" to Ms. Marvelous. He lit up for the first time that morning and delivered an emphatic, "Yes!"

The three of us followed the long corridor back to his first grade classroom. The assistant teacher immediately came over and hugged Ricochet. Ms. Marvelous was talking with other parents, but came right over when she was free and hugged him, too. Although he was still hiding behind me a bit, they were able to talk with him for a while about his summer and his new teacher. I noticed an envelope with Ricochet's name on it on the table next to us — an unassuming, plain white envelope with his name carefully hand-printed in black ink. The assistant teacher handed the envelope to Ricochet on our way out.

"This is a special note from Ms. Marvelous that she wrote just for you," she offered with a wink.

I was so anxious to know what this great teacher had done that I asked him to read it in the car before we left the school parking lot. It was a typed note on a simple sheet of plain copy paper.

"This is too much for me to read. You read it!" He was still acting bashful, and he always resisted reading.

"Hand it to me, and I'll read it out loud," I said with my hand outstretched to the back seat.

I read from the beginning:

Dear [Ricochet],
This is a special letter just for you to keep somewhere in your desk or backpack.

Tears were instant. The thought quickly crossed my mind that I might not be able to read him the entire letter without spewing emotion.

When you feel a little nervous or scared or not sure about things, take this letter out and read Mrs. M's reasons why you are so special!
- *You are very kind to everyone!*
- *You have a great smile that makes people feel better!*
- *You are very bright and smart!*

- *You can do anything you set your mind to!*
- *You make Mrs. M and Mrs. T smile!*

I love you!
Mrs. M

My voice was cracking a bit by the time I reached the end and tears dripped from my chin. Ricochet was behind me in the back seat and oblivious to my emotional reaction. I peeked up in the rearview mirror to catch a glimpse of his proud, bright smile. What special women these two teachers are! They understood Ricochet so completely. I was so very grateful he experienced teachers who cared this much about him.

Ms. Marvelous, you are one in a million, lady. Truly, truly a gift!

Second grade begins

The first day of school in the fall of 2009 was like silk on sandpaper. It was an isolating experience for Ricochet, and Warrior Girl cried for two hours that afternoon because she didn't have any friends in her class, and no one befriended her all day, either. It could only get smoother, I hoped, and it did. We ended that first week nearly on a high note.

Ricochet's new teacher, Ms. Glinda, had been doing everything she could to try to follow his 504 accommodations and ensure her classroom was an environment in which he could learn. Her enthusiasm was contagious. However, many of the strategies she implemented were overkill and more detrimental than beneficial.

When I walked Ricochet into school the first morning, I found that she had given him his own "office," as she called it. He had two desks all to himself and a large area taped off around it — he had his own corner of the room. She even had several table-top games nearby to use as fidgets. When I considered the special needs of a child with ADHD and their often fragile self-confidence, I realized everything she'd done to make him comfortable in her classroom wasn't ideal at all.

First, isolating a child isn't good. Ricochet was removed from his peers, whose desks were grouped together in the center of the room. He was alone and separated, and he knew it and felt it immediately.

With this far-removed placement, he couldn't see the teacher's face when she was talking to the class. Eye-contact can be crucial, and I don't think he processed much of anything Ms. Glinda said that first day.

The items she gave him as fidget tools were actual toys and a further distraction. Not only a distraction for Ricochet, but the other kids were gathering around his desk to check out what he had that they didn't. He needed a stress ball or therapy putty for hand manipulation while listening to the lessons, not something that would fully deplete his already waning attention.

With all this hijacking my thoughts, I marched into the classroom with Ricochet thirty minutes before class started the second morning. I expressed my concerns to Ms. Glinda about the isolating placement, and kindly told her Ricochet was expressing concern about not being part of the group as well. I also let her know he had a hard time hearing from where he was sitting. She immediately offered to do whatever she needed to make him comfortable, and expressed that she hoped I realized she only wanted what was best for him. I did realize that, and I confirmed it by conveying my appreciation for all the effort she was putting into doing just that. I offered to come back after school to help her move the furniture and desks in the classroom. She decided she wanted to go ahead and do it right then before class started. I think it bothered her that he was unhappy. I loved that — not that it was bothering her, but that her focus was comfortable students.

And so we moved classroom furniture at 7:40 AM that morning as the students trickled in and settled. I was sweating by the time I left. While his placement still wasn't my ideal, it addressed the most crucial and immediate deficiencies. He was still off to the side, but right up to the edge of the grouped desks with the rest of the class. He could see her face when she addressed the class then, and he was with the group.

I planned to observe and help in the classroom the following week to see how things were going for Ricochet. I was determined to help my little boy succeed.

The day ADHD defeated me

As that fall progressed, a dark place rose up quietly and engulfed me from behind. Ricochet's developmental specialist was inaccessible. It was like trying to penetrate Fort Knox to be able to speak to him outside a scheduled appointment, and his schedule was booked at least three months out. When I had a medication issue, I had to leave a voice-mail for a nurse. Sometimes she called me to discuss, sometimes not. She then typed up a message with a summary of my concerns for the doctor via in-house messaging. Then, when he had time, he sent her a reply message, and she then called me back. Very rarely did even the nurse and the doctor discuss our problems, and never was I be able to talk with the doctor without an appointment.

I felt trapped into seeing this doctor for Ricochet's ADHD care. He was *the* doctor for ADHD in our area. Pediatric developmental delays were his specialty. I was told no one in town knew more about this than he did. No one else in town treated ADHD outside a mental health practice either, so this was the only doctor Ricochet could see for ADHD under our insurance.

We saw this doctor for almost a year, and his inaccessibility always bothered me. My discomfort with his care came to a head when we had yet another medication problem and couldn't get an answer about it for two weeks. I was irritated, but the regular phone nurse was on vacation, and I had never had to wait so long before, so I overlooked it at first. When they finally answered me, it was that first day of a second grade. I tapered the dose of the blood pressure medication as instructed, but one and a half weeks into the taper, Ricochet's behavior was generally worse than it had been before he began taking medication for ADHD.

I called again and explained that I couldn't accept medications making my son's behavior worse, rather than better. I received a phone call back the next day, instructing me to stop the stimulant, Medication #3, for two weeks, but to continue to give him half the dose of the secondary medication. Then his teacher was to fill out their evaluation form so they could see "what is really helping." In other words, they thought I was overreacting and that this would remind me what life was like before treatment. This was a move to appease me because I had told the nurse honestly that I wasn't okay with giving my child medication that was making life worse for him and everyone around him. I was scared to death to stop the stimulant and send him to school, though. I felt like I was setting him up to fail.

The developmental specialist also suggested we go to counseling so I could learn how to deal with Ricochet's behaviors. I told the phone nurse half a dozen times that it wasn't that I couldn't handle his behavior, it was that I couldn't handle giving him medication that *caused his behavior to be worse.* Mr. T and I only gave him ADHD medication to offer academic success; I never suspected anything was wrong with him before he started school! I was a great mom who put far more effort into managing his special needs than many others would. I didn't ever feel I might harm Ricochet, or anything else they were insinuating.

I decided to change medication as he suggested and see what happened. I knew the first day without Medication #3 — without any stimulant at all for the first time in nine months — was not going to be easy. Fortunately, I didn't realize how bad it could be or I wouldn't have gotten out of bed that morning.

Ricochet was an obnoxious, arrogant, spiteful, embarrassing disaster on the low dose of blood pressure medication alone. He continually made loud noises, and was very rude to any and all who dared to speak to him, including me. He kicked his desk from underneath like a gong simply to be disruptive, even after being asked repeatedly to stop. The student teacher had to sit with him to do his work, although he didn't do anything but make her second-guess her career choice.

I sat behind him and cut out some bulletin board decorations for his teacher. I wanted to see how he'd behave without me holding his hand and, frankly, how the school would handle it. It was all I could do not to cry. It was brutal watching him behave in such a foreign manner. I did not know this new little boy.

After only an hour and a half into the school day, I walked outside and called the doctor. I wasn't going to tolerate turning my sweet but mischievous boy into an unrecognizable monster. I didn't call his developmental specialist's office though, the one who had prescribed and guided the medicine for the last year, including this failure of a change. Instead, I called our regular pediatrician where I could get an appointment and talk with an actual doctor the same day.

It was 9:30 AM at that point, and our appointment wasn't until 11:30 AM, but I marched straight to the front office and signed Ricochet out of school. He was only making everyone miserable and preventing his classmates from getting any work done. Plus, I needed time to go back through my journaling and document all the medications, dosages, side effects, etc. from the beginning for our pediatrician.

I wish I could say the pediatrician saved the day. He did not. But he sure wanted to, and that felt great. He said he wished he could write a new prescription or have new wisdom to give us an immediate fix to our situation. He explained that he was outside his comfort zone and didn't know enough about ADHD and ADHD medications to truly guide us in a positive direction. He was happy to refer us to a new specialist, though.

We talked about the fact that referring us to any type of mental health practice would cost more than we could afford due to inadequate insurance. I couldn't possibly scrape up the funds to pay for frequent doctor visits out of pocket. I was already accumulating credit card debt paying copays for Ricochet's occupational therapy.

The pediatrician decided he would consult with their in-house counselor on resources she recommended to her patients with ADHD. He promised to find a new specialist for us who would be covered by our insurance and who would be accessible when we had medication problems and other concerns that couldn't wait for three-month checkups. I would hear from him the following week.

In the meantime, he said Ricochet could go back to the last medications and dosages that made his ADHD manageable until he could see a new specialist. I wished I had never stirred the pot away from that at his last checkup with the developmental specialist a couple of weeks prior. Other than a couple of meltdowns, it was going fine. I wondered if the perfectionist in me and my need to make everything better for my children lead me to over-analyze something that was working pretty well. Did I sabotage things inadvertently? Whether I did or not, it was going to be good to have a fresh pair of eyes analyzing our situation and Ricochet's needs.

Ricochet did get better as that day went on, too. I think his (big, smart) brain was so used to having the help of Medication #3 that it was a scrambled mess that morning without it. After a few hours, he began to acclimate. I gave him a full blood pressure medicine tablet that afternoon to get back on track as quickly as possible, even though he hadn't had a stimulant that day. It was actually a great afternoon. He and Warrior Girl got along famously and played together, without fighting, for several hours. Then he spent time in the garage with Mr. T, building. I didn't hear one raised voice the entire time.

A broken heart really is contagious

I felt weary at this point in my journey learning to parent a child with ADHD. I was stuck in a perpetual state of sadness. Many medications had failed, Ricochet's teachers didn't understand him and his academic needs, and I was beginning to finally realize and accept there's no "fix" for ADHD.

I tried to focus on the positive. I tried to hurry along all the work we needed to put in to catch our tailwind and get to that better place. I tried to continue to believe that this better place — that elusive "place" where we could get through an entire day without thinking about ADHD — existed. Each time I succeeded in feeling positive again, another disappointment would swoop in and steal my optimism. I found myself feeling so sorry for my little man frequently and consistently for several months. So much in his life was all wrong, and I desperately needed to make it better.

I thought things were finally looking up when Ricochet was invited to a classmate's birthday party at the roller-skating rink. It was very important that he had the opportunity to build friendships, so I rearranged our schedule so he could attend the party. He was excited about it, so I found myself excited about it, too.

When we got to the rink, the birthday boy's dad came right up, introduced himself, and got Ricochet a pair of skates. *We're off to a great start.* We laced up the skates while he watched his friends glide around the rink with confident speed. Then he stood up and fell right back on his butt. He saw the other boys skating and was confused as to why he couldn't just stand up, go out there, and skate, too.

He stood up again, completely determined, and stepped off the carpet and onto the rink. I, of course, hovered beside him, holding his hand. He couldn't remain vertical for even a second. We got back on the carpet, and he skated back and forth there, trying to get the hang of it. He literally fell every foot or two. Every time he fell, he put his arms down to catch himself. He began to go several feet without holding onto me before falling, and I thought he might learn to skate after all. Then he fell one more time, hands first and lay on the floor, crying in pain. That was the end of skating for Ricochet.

"Get these skates off me!" he yelled. "I'm never skating again. I can't do it like they can!"

"It takes lots of practice to be able to skate, sweetie," I answered, as gingerly as I could. Not only was his arm hurt, but his self-esteem was badly bruised as well. "Your friends have been skating before to be that good at it today, but this is your first time."

His tears multiplied.

We put his tennis shoes back on and got a bag of ice for his wrist. He sat at a table and cried for a good twenty minutes. I was a little worried he had broken his arm, but he finally stopped crying and started moving it some — he was favoring it and wincing, but he was moving it.

And yet, he did not want to leave the party.

He laid his head down on the table and cried intermittently for the next thirty minutes. He was so disappointed that he was hurt and couldn't participate in skating with the other kids.

The boys left the rink and began to gather in the area where Ricochet was sulking. I hoped cake would brighten things up for him. No such luck. He scooted in on the bench by the birthday boy... and the birthday boy wanted someone else to sit by him. Ricochet fought for the spot he rightfully claimed first, but he lost. The other boy climbed over him, still in roller skates, and bashed Ricochet's shin with his skate. Injuries #2 (emotional) and #3 (bruised shin) had occurred.

I told Ricochet I'd give him one dollar to play video games when the boys went back out to skate. I had offered to help him skate again, but he wasn't going to put wheels on his feet again that day — maybe ever. I thought a couple video games would take his mind off it, so we got quarters and he tried a racing machine. Broken. Then he put a quarter in another racing machine. Also, apparently, broken. He put his last quarter in a pinball machine to find out it required two quarters. Of course, his eyes welled up with tears and he began to cry again. I went to the staff, but they wouldn't give refunds because they didn't own the machines. I was out of cash.

Ricochet just broke down. His broken heart was Injury #4.

He was ready to leave the party at that point, barely more than halfway through. I was certainly ready to stop seeing him hurt, so I agreed. On the way out, he was crying so hard that the girl working the door reached into her pocket, pulled out two dollars, and gave them to him. I tried to tell her we only lost one dollar in the machines and it wasn't necessary for her to give him money, but she insisted and I couldn't stand to break his heart more.

We got in the car and I started it up. Ricochet said to me, "Momma, if I get invited to another roller-skating party, I'm not going. I'm never going to skate again."

My fearless, impulsive little boy was giving up on something forever. That was big.

He decided right away that he wanted to give Warrior Girl one of his dollars. He spent the other on a Mountain Dew at the grocery store. I would normally refuse Mountain Dew, but I wasn't about to break his heart again. I think I would have let him drink red Gatorade at that moment, a huge no-no for Ricochet. That Mountain Dew was going to make the rotten day a little better for him, and I needed that almost as much as he did.

I don't ride roller coasters

The start of the new school year was a much bigger upheaval than I imagined. Ricochet's medications weren't ideal, *again*. I was looking for a new specialist for his ADHD treatment and management. He was nearing the end of occupational therapy, and I couldn't figure out how to continue it financially. Mr. T and I were making a huge push to complete all the work on our house by spring to get it on the market and move across town. I was at the breaking point with my real estate career — I had to close a sale within the next thirty to forty-five days or find a new job. Mr. T was overloaded between work, teaching weekend woodworking classes, and playing co-ed softball in the evenings. There was a lot of change.

I was not averse to change, recognizing that change is the only path to improvement. I welcomed positive change.

These changes were like a roller coaster with a lot of ups and downs and a few neck-jerking turns. I have never been a fan of roller coasters. All was unsettled. But, once we found our groove again, I knew it would be even better than before the upheaval. I had my eyes out of the muck and on the prize.

Ricochet and I went to see a child therapist at the behavioral health office recommended by our pediatrician. I was aware our insurance would not cover visits to a therapist, and that this office required regular visits with their therapists to have a patient on ADHD medications. I went for an initial visit to find out how often we'd have to come in (and pay out of pocket) and if we could see the behavioral pediatrician on staff sometimes so insurance would cover some of it.

The therapist was wonderful and eager to work with us. She recognized after ten minutes with Ricochet that "his meds really aren't working." The policy was that we had to come in weekly until he was "stable" and then every eight to twelve weeks as needed. She outlined a schedule to proceed: we were to go back to her the next week, and then see the behavioral pediatrician the week after for medication change. I scheduled the appointments, and then called the insurance company. I came to find out that the insurance company didn't care that he was an MD; because he worked in a mental health office, he was a mental health provider under the guidelines of our policy. That meant visits to him were also subject to our annual $5,000 mental health deductible. That meant we didn't have insurance coverage for anyone in their office.

I swiped the phone off my desk in disappointment-fueled anger, and immediately cancelled the appointments with the new therapist and behavioral pediatrician. While the idea of consistent and frequent monitoring of Ricochet's medication and general guidance on living with ADHD was ideal, getting a bill for $500 a month for ADHD care was anything but. We didn't have an extra $500 each month anyway.

I was also enraged that ADHD, a neurological disorder, was primarily treated by mental health professionals. I couldn't make sense of that. If it were a brain tumor affecting behavior, a neurologist would treat it and it would be covered by insurance with a simple copay. But a chemical issue in the brain is classified as mental? I certainly saw the benefits of therapy for managing ADHD, but felt the day-to-day treatment should be managed by an MD, such as a neurologist.

All that work to find better treatment for Ricochet, and we were still in limbo-land. I had a professional second opinion that Ricochet's medications weren't working, but I still didn't have anyone to help fix it. Our general pediatrician was still working to find a solution, but the prospects were slim.

With the encouragement of the therapist we visited, I applied for our state children's health insurance plan. Our income was right on the line of eligibility, but my business had a loss that year so our family should qualify. If approved, that would provide both kids one year of full health, mental health, dental, vision, and therapy services at very little cost. I felt euphoric just thinking about it. Unfortunately, it would take as much as thirty days to find out if we were approved.

There were some wonderful possibilities on the horizon. If I could just get his medicine changed and feel more confident about his experience at school, I could relax again. I had to believe it would work out!

A profound shift

ADHD medications were no longer effective, and I was exasperated with Ricochet's doctor, trying to get him to "hear me" and make a change. That debacle was all-consuming for a while.

In all the renewed chaos of hyperactivity and inattention, characteristics that usually inhibit learning and general school success, Ricochet skyrocketed academically. It was a profound shift I spent many hours pondering, but couldn't understand — there was nothing I could attribute it to. His medications weren't managing his activity level or improving focus. Ms. Glinda, while loving and willing to make accommodations for him, was not giving him extra or differentiated instruction. I had even been pretty lax on homework, doing the bare minimum to keep frustration as low as possible. At occupational therapy, they stopped working on handwriting, and focused on behavior modification, sensory issues, and auditory processing. We had not increased academic instruction or even tried anything terribly different.

And yet, the light came on and shone brightly for Ricochet. He received a perfect score on his spelling tests three weeks in a row. He tested at Level M on their reading scale, but had barely scored a Level I three months before. I didn't even read much with him the previous summer, wanting him to be creative and free and have a break from all the "work" that tormented him.

In addition to this positive, inexplicable shift in academics, he also made a seemingly overnight improvement in his drawing. He went from scribbling and mediocre stick figures without any color (he refused color, or stuck with only one per drawing), to drawing a full story with scenery and everything, in full color and so clear that I could tell what everything was without asking. I noted a complete 180-degree turn from the pictures he created just two weeks before.

I found this inexplicable. I studied his situation with medication not working, a new classroom and teacher, and a battle with the doctor and expected the complete opposite outcome. My logical mind was totally baffled, but my heart was filled with joy!

Recognizing that failure is a part of life for everyone

As I watched the final game between the Yankees and the Angels to decide who was going to play the Phillies in the 2009 World Series, I found myself comparing the game of baseball to my life. I realized there is a strong correlation between life and baseball, especially when parenting a special needs child.

Think what life would be like if we employed the "three strikes and you're out" rule.

I punished my son for behaviors out of his control before he was diagnosed with ADHD. STRIKE 1

I lost my temper with my son when he laughed in my face when I was very serious. STRIKE 2

I lost the battle with the local school system to have my son included in Special Education. STRIKE 3

If I played my life like a game of baseball, I would be "out" in the 2nd inning, long before the game was over. But when a player strikes out in baseball, they get another chance again and again — they're only out for a short time.

Professional baseball players understand that a strike-out is a common part of the game, not a sign of failure. Statistically, they get out when up to bat far more than they take a base. They don't let a previous strike-out affect their game in the present moment. They get back up to the plate and employ their skill, determination, and positive attitude to succeed the next time they are up to bat. If a strike-out defeated them, they'd never get a hit and succeed.

A moment of weakness is not a sign of failure. A failure of my child's is not necessarily a failure of my own either. It is especially crucial to remember that when parenting a special needs child. Some of Ricochet's "failures" were just part of his genetic code and not really failures at all.

I was the first to admit I often felt like I was failing my children. I had to keep that attitude in check though — going down that rabbit hole was exactly how I *could* actually fail my children. It was crucial to continue to refocus on the goal. I had to keep my eye on the prize. I needed to visualize myself hitting that home run and crossing home plate.

As I watched some of these men hit nearly a dozen foul balls in one at bat that night, I marveled at their determination to stay in the game. Their determination to keep swinging, to get a hit, and to stay on the field. They were making contact with the ball, the first step to getting a hit. They just needed to adjust a little — straighten up their swing, or swing a hair earlier or a smidge later. They were on the right track. They almost had it. They weren't giving up... and neither should I.

5
A New Beginning

"You raze the old to raise the new."
— Justina Chen, North of Beautiful

Starting from scratch

There are two types of stimulant medications for ADHD: methylphenidate and amphetamine. Each type works differently for different people. The developmental specialist had actually listened to me at our last check-up and changed Ricochet from Medicine #3, a methylphenidate, to Medication #4, an amphetamine-based medication. I witnessed an amazing improvement in Ricochet's behavior the first few days, but angry and aggressive behavior grew worse and worse until Medication #4 became intolerable. He was also a completely out-of-control, wild, smug, sarcastic, and disrespectful "devil-child" in the mornings. He gave the term "wild thing" a whole new meaning. He was very spiteful and mean. He refused to get dressed, brush his teeth, eat breakfast, and anything and everything

I instructed. He laughed in my face with every single direction. He developed this new, high-pitched squeal of a yell, which he employed every time I threatened punishment for not following directions. He knew it hurt my ears and knew, more effectively, that I couldn't talk over it. It made for extremely miserable mornings.

I hadn't been happy with the treatment provided by the developmental doctor who diagnosed Ricochet pretty much from the first appointment. Late that fall the kids were approved for state insurance that covered mental health, and we immediately dumped the developmental specialist and switched to the new behavioral health practice that offered a therapist and a behavioral pediatrician.

About the time I was ready to throw my hands up, we had Ricochet's first appointment with the new therapist who would be managing his ADHD care. She was baffled by the outrageous morning behavior with Medication #4 and witnessed the afternoon lull in coverage, too. When we arrived at her office, he was hyper, demanding, and not paying a lick of attention to anything anyone said to him. That happened from about two o'clock until four or five every day. Our appointment was at four, but she intentionally kept us late to see that lull in medication efficacy. At about 4:45 PM, he started to settle. He sat next to me on the sofa, but his feet were up over his head and flailing around — he was still very fidgety. By five o'clock, though, he was sitting up properly, still and engaged in our conversation. The therapist was in awe. She didn't know what to make of it since Medication #4 was supposed to be the most high-tech, evenly-released stimulant medication on the market.

"It's obvious his medication isn't working," she concluded. "I'm really frustrated by this, and ADHD is my specialty. I can't imagine how frustrating it must be to be his parent in this situation."

I nodded.

While she was only a therapist and couldn't prescribe medication, she hinted about stopping Medication #4 to see what happened. The next morning, a Friday, Ricochet did not have Medication #4. He did still take the blood pressure medication since we couldn't stop it cold turkey without potentially causing blood pressure irregularity. She talked to the behavioral pediatrician in their office directly Friday morning, and had him squeeze us into his schedule at noon the following Monday so we could get Ricochet's medications straightened out.

Until then, there was a fierce battle of wills and a lot of tears. Ricochet had been completely mean and uncontrollable, an absolute nightmare like I'd never before experienced. I was reduced to tears at least three times a day. He acted almost like a drug addict having withdrawals or something. He wasn't at all himself.

At our Monday appointment, our first visit with this doctor, I asked the nagging question the behavioral specialist couldn't answer, "Why does this stimulant give super-great results for a couple of months and then fail? Is he metabolizing it too fast? Should I give it independent of breakfast? Or maybe after breakfast instead of before? Is there anything I can do differently to make it effective again?"

"I'm afraid I can't answer that," he said, in his restrained, but sophisticated southern drawl. He didn't know why either. But, at least he didn't tell me I had to settle for mediocre treatment. He had us try other medications.

I spent over an hour with him, going back over all the experiences and medication trials thus far. He agreed that Medication #4 was the wrong medication for Ricochet, and that the amphetamine-based medications in general were not right for him. He gave me the option of going back to Medication #3 and meeting every three to four weeks to try to make it work long-term (since it had worked well at times), or to try Medication #5, which we hadn't tried yet. I decided to go back to Medication #3, by itself, and then work with the new doctor to try to make it work. We knew Medication #3 was very effective with few side effects when it worked. The only problem was that it lost effectiveness after a month or two. We had bumped the dosage up once before, but the same thing occurred. Ricochet began the last dosage he had been on of Medication #3. After Thanksgiving, we would go back to the doctor and evaluate how things were going to make any adjustments needed at that time. In the meantime, the therapist would keep weekly tabs on him in counseling.

New treatment and new treatment providers was like starting from scratch, and starting from scratch could be good. I wasn't sure if wiping the slate clean and starting over after a year of ADHD medication trials was the good kind of starting from scratch, though. It felt like an opportunity, but I knew it was going to be rough, at least at first.

Beginning true behavior management

It was apparent from the beginning that Ricochet's therapist was going to hold me accountable. She would make sure I created and maintained the best possible environment for Ricochet, but also for Warrior Girl, as a sibling of ADHD. It was her job to teach Mr. T and me the strategies and tools available to effectively parent a child with ADHD. It was sure to be a lot of work, but I was looking forward to finally implementing systems and controlling the reins. ADHD had been controlling us for a long time, and it was time we restored proper balance.

Each weekly session would start with the good and the bad from the week, and then she would share ideas for managing and resolving any issues we had. What a blessing that was going to be for me!

On our second visit, she advised me to limit screen time. That was a biggie. When I broke down and introduced the computer and Nintendo to my kids originally, I had big plans that included time limits and digital timers. I got lazy, it became time-consuming and difficult to manage, and I gave up. I always rationalized that we lived where the kids couldn't just run outside to play because of the bears, so I let them have more screen time to fill that "void." There were plenty of things to do besides screen time though, and I had to stop taking the easy route and regain control.

My homework assignment from the therapist was to create the reward system and limit screen time, and then

I had to report back to her that they were accomplished. I knew there wasn't a punishment for not completing a task she had assigned, but it sure was nice to not have to figure things out for myself and more motivating to have to sit face-to-face and potentially admit I didn't do my very best.

When I broke the news of a new behavior system on the horizon to Warrior Girl later that day, she was angry. It was going to be very difficult to change a free-for-all system that had been in place her entire ten years! I think that's why I never implemented token and reward systems when I read about them when researching ADHD. It was really late in the game to be changing things on her, but the changes were good for her, too. I hoped she'd realize that someday.

Of course, Ricochet was upset about the limits as well. He frequently pestered the life out of me until I gave in and let him break the limits. I taught him that by giving in so often. I wished I hadn't.

I often trump things up in my mind, anticipating possible negative outcomes and imagining the situation to be much worse than it actually turns out to be. This was true of the full implementation of our rewards system. I had imagined such anarchy from my kids that I put off implementing a system for over a year. Now that I was accountable to Ricochet's new therapist, I could no longer rest on excuses.

I didn't start with the full-on, everything is earned, nothing is a right other than food and shelter approach as the therapist suggested. That was too much of a change all at once for children who were set in their ways of controlling me! I gave them a small amount of TV, computer, and video game time each day. They could earn bonuses and other things off a menu of activities, or they could lose their basic privileges as negative consequences for unacceptable behavior.

I purchased poker chips and collection jars for each kid that week. I let Ricochet and Warrior Girl decorate their jars so they had some ownership of the new system. I created a rewards menu, which was a list of how they could spend their tokens and what the rewards would cost, and posted it on the wall above where their collection jars sat on the kitchen counter.

I was able to give Ricochet a few tokens here and there over the first week. I also had the opportunity to take tokens away. It was a bit harder for Warrior Girl to earn tokens since she had to have a good attitude and refrain from back-sassing to be eligible, a tough standard for any tween.

This new system was tough for me, too. I couldn't get work done, talk on the phone, do laundry, or clean when I had to entertain my children. Besides computer, Nintendo, and TV, they didn't initiate any other play on their own, other than Ricochet building with Legos. I envisioned a life where I stood over top of them every waking hour to enforce the limits I always wanted. It seemed more torturous for me than for them.

But I was not a wimp, and I didn't back down (much). I set the following limits:

- 1.5 hours max screen time each (Nintendo, TV, or computer/Internet)

- chores must be done before tokens can be spent on any rewards
- whenever I get to "three" when I am counting for compliance, it is a token lost — no bargaining, no exceptions
- all kid stuff must be put in its proper place before going to bed.

Medication #3 was not working much at all *again* by this time, so I braced for a battle. I believed that, if we could survive the transition, the motivation that needing to earn privileges instills would improve behavior and life in our house would be easier and happier. At that point, I was hoping for mere survival, though.

Ricochet and Warrior Girl both really surprised me. Warrior Girl back-sassed the new system when signing up for time slots for screen activities at first, but only the first few days. She and Ricochet both did well with it. In fact, they did so well that, after the first three days, they were already finding alternatives to screen time independently.

They were dressed, fed, and ready for school about twenty minutes early the third morning after I implemented the system, a real marvel in and of itself. Where they would usually turn to the TV or electronics to pass that time, they were instead having a Nerf Blaster battle together. The TV was off, and they were even getting along. My jaw was on the floor. I should have given my crazy munchkins more credit — they did sometimes choose the right thing! They both earned a token that morning for getting up, dressing, and eating when I asked them to.

We would have ups and downs, as we always did, but implementation of the full behavior management system went far better than I imagined.

The great snow of 2009

Here in Asheville, we get small snowfalls a handful of times throughout each winter. Usually, it's a dusting to an inch in town and melts by midday. Up on our mountain, we typically saw one to three inches and only got snowed in once each winter season. But in December of 2009, we had the "Great Snow of 2009" — the media's title, although I agreed wholeheartedly. Eighteen inches of snow accumulated on our property, the most in the prior decade for Asheville. While it slowed down the city folk for a couple days until roads and parking lots could be plowed, our lives froze in time on the mountain. We were snowed in.

At first, it was no biggie. I was having fun playing out in the snow with the kids. We rarely saw snow stacked on tree branches because we usually had a lot of wind at our elevation, but it was calm and still and the branches were turning a powdery white. It was beautiful.

Before long, I was enamored with snow no more. It was 5:30 PM Friday, the sun was setting, and our power went out. Mr. T and I knew immediately that the power would be out for an extended period of time. This was not a typical snowfall, and it was not business as usual for the power company to make repairs this time. Snow and I were no longer friends.

It made for quite the survival adventure, right in our home. We had gas logs in our fireplace and a propane tank to fuel it, so we had heat in the great room. We all hunkered down in the living room to sleep together on the floor and sofa in front of the fire. For four days, we each wore long johns, sweatpants, two shirts, a sweater, and our coats and hats day and night inside our house. We slept under many blankets.

A well supplied water to our house. That is, when we had electricity it did. We weren't ready for an emergency and didn't have any bottled water at the house. Our water supply ran out before we went to sleep the first day. We had a gas cooktop on our range so we boiled snow into water for all sorts of things: to flush toilets, wash dishes, make soup out of leftover chicken, make iced tea, boil spaghetti, etc. Boiling snow was a constant, all day job. We had a large stock pot that Mr. T would fill up with snow, piled above the rim of the pot. Once melted, there would be little more than an inch of water in the bottom. I never realized how many gallons of water a day a person uses until we were boiling it an inch at a time.

The days and nights were long without entertainment. We were able to charge the kids' Nintendos in my car in the garage, and that helped, but they were antsy and bored, especially when darkness fell each night. We played board games by flashlight, but that never lasted past 7 or 8 PM. One can only play Sorry so many times in a row. We didn't want to burn up all the flashlight batteries too quickly, either. The kids usually went to bed at eight, and they were still on that schedule. But Mr. T and I had to lie down when they did... there wasn't anything else to do in the cold darkness.

Warrior Girl's anxiety got the best of her, and she panicked at times. I explained to her that we'd hike down the mountain and go somewhere else if our home became unsafe. That helped, but she still woke up each morning in despair — devastated that the day would be a repeat of the one before. I awoke feeling the same on Sunday morning, the start of day three without power. I was tired of the situation and ready for a change.

On Monday morning, the power came on, four days after it had gone out. Cheering and screaming, jumping and whooping could be heard throughout our house. I don't recall us ever cheering as a family like that before. Having the power back was spectacular, but we were still stuck on the mountain, and we had very little food left since the majority spoiled while the power was off. Mr. T tried to dig a path for my car, but it was too much for one man, one snow shovel, and a half mile of eighteen-inch deep snow. I helped for a bit, but once the power came back on, I needed to get things back in order inside.

Mr. T had parked his car about a half-mile down the mountain that Friday morning when he returned to find the snow had already accumulated too much to drive all the way up to our house. So on Monday, he hiked down to his car and went to the grocery for food, buying only as much as he could fit in a backpack for the half-mile return hike. He hiked out a couple more times that week for food and actually scored some chains for his tires (every store in town was sold out of chains, snow boots, and waterproof gloves by the time he finally got out). A week after the snow fell, he was finally able to drive his car all the way up to our house with chains on all four tires. Two days after that, I was finally able to drive my car out and went shopping. I just had to get off the mountain and out of the house after being snowed in for eight days!

I had expected an unpredictable and foreign situation like this to exacerbate ADHD. Routine is crucial to keep ADHD under control, and our routine that week was out the window. Snow play got old really quickly, and it was so hard to warm up afterward with only a fireplace to heat the house. There wasn't much activity to be had for our hyperactive child. Having something available Ricochet was used to, his Nintendo, gave him a small tie to normalcy and did surprisingly well throughout the ordeal. His behavior was topnotch, actually.

I abandoned our token system during the snow, and decided not to bother with it until life returned to normal and the kids got back to school. We missed many of Ricochet's ADHD care appointments, too: a checkup for medication, new evaluation testing, counseling, and occupational therapy. After a few weeks, we were back to the same school routine and our family's version of normal. What a surprising adventure that was.

The year we almost let ADHD ruin our Christmas

Impulsivity is a hallmark of ADHD. Mr. T and I know that all too well. Most mornings up to this point, Ricochet was up before anyone else hunting for the cookies, chocolate, and candy and eating as much of it as he could shovel in before anyone else woke. He found and accessed all our hiding places. Even the top shelf of the pantry, about eight feet up, was accessible to him by climbing the shelves like a ladder.

In light of this experience, Mr. T decided he would sleep on the couch by the Christmas tree the night Santa leaves the presents, but I didn't want my husband sleeping on the couch on Christmas Eve. I gave Mr. T a good coaching. "We have to give Ricochet the benefit of the doubt. If we set some pretty strict consequences, he will wake us before going downstairs. I don't want you sleeping on the couch for Christmas." My tone had a touch of pleading.

We motioned Ricochet and Warrior Girl over. "Anything you open without Momma and Daddy will not be yours; it will be taken away from you," Mr. T explained.

What kid wants their Christmas presents taken away after they open them? My plan was foolproof.

Mr. T and I were both upstairs in our bed, enjoying our long winter's nap while St. Nick made his magic in our living room. Suddenly, Warrior Girl was standing over me in a panic, muttering about how Ricochet was downstairs opening his presents. I sprung from my bed. The time was 4:30 AM. Down the stairs I flew, desperate to keep him from opening the "big surprise gift." That would surely ruin Christmas.

I rounded the corner into the living room and there was Ricochet, sitting on the floor, a Lego set and his R2-D2 mini-figure on the ottoman before him. The Lego box was already open and scattered. My heart sank to my stomach in an instant. Disappointment was written all over my face and oozing from my tone as I addressed him.

"What are you doing? You know you were not supposed to open anything without getting me or Daddy! I am so disappointed in you, Ricochet. What did we say would happen if you opened presents without us?" It all just spilled from my lips. He was lucky I was still half-asleep, or it would have been a much longer rant.

"You will take them away," Ricochet said with a falling bottom lip. "I am so stupid!" he shouted.

My heart broke into a million pieces right then and there. I was angry with him for disobeying the rules, yet it had been so likely that he would do so that Mr. T wanted to sleep on the sofa and guard the presents. Now my heart hurt for Ricochet because the consequences of his actions finally hit him. He was disappointed in himself and his lack of self-control. At the age of seven, he saw it as stupidity. He didn't really understand that he has a condition that prevents him from being able to control his actions sometimes. And he hadn't yet learned to work around his troubled neurology.

I quickly gathered up the items he had opened, turning away from him as my eyes filled with tears. I didn't want him to feel worse by seeing my sadness. It was the way he felt about himself in that moment that had made me cry.

We put away the toys and turned out the lights, and I climbed into Ricochet's bed with him. It wasn't even five o'clock yet, much too early to get up and start the day, Christmas or not. We lay there for about two hours. I asked for the impossible, begging him to lie still in tired desperation. The more he wiggled, the more frustrated I became. Neither Ricochet nor I ever went back to sleep. By 6:45 AM, I was tired of asking him to lie still and distraught that I wasn't going to sleep more.

I knew Mr. T was fuming mad about what had happened — mad at Ricochet for breaking the rules, and mad at me for not letting him sleep on the sofa to prevent it. I went in and asked if we could go ahead and get up and start our Christmas morning routine. Mr. T was not having it. He did not want to get up before seven. He also wanted to teach Ricochet a lesson by postponing the festivities. He didn't say it outright, but I knew that was what he was thinking.

I began yelling, "We are all angry, and Christmas is already totally ruined, so why not just get up and get it over with so we can move on with the day?"

Get Christmas "over with"?

I brushed my teeth, put on my slippers and sweater, and prepared for presents. Mr. T saw that he wasn't going to get more sleep, so he got up too. He bumped and slammed around the kitchen and took out his frustrations on the coffee machine.

As I listened to all the over-dramatic signs of his anger, I realized that he didn't understand that Ricochet truly couldn't help but open those presents. The thought was in Ricochet's mind, and the apparatus that told him to wait doesn't work so well. He must not have known that Ricochet was feeling worse than awful, too.

I turned to Mr. T, and began shouting, "You don't understand him at all. You don't understand that he physically can't stop himself. You don't get it. You don't get him. He actually said he was 'stupid' and cried when

I found him. If you don't get him, I don't want you in this house!" I reached a full-blown, belly-aching cry by the end of my outburst.

I fled into the pantry to fall apart away from the kids. They were already feeling guilty and ashamed, and the longer I stood in there sobbing and crying, the more I realized our reaction was far out of scale for the offense. So he opened a couple presents. Big deal. He didn't ruin the big surprise. In fact, when I thought about it, it was cute that he was down there at four-thirty in the morning, so excited about Christmas.

We were disappointed that he couldn't control himself, that we missed his reaction when he opened those presents, and that things didn't go according to plan. We were disappointed he has ADHD when you boil it down to the truth of the matter. Somewhere between my uncontrollable sobbing in the pantry, Ricochet's whimpering in the living room, and Warrior Girl's anxious expression, Mr. T also realized it wasn't worth all the drama and certainly wasn't worth ruining Christmas.

Mr. T approached me and apologized, and I was finally able to compose myself. I retrieved my camera, and we all gathered around the tree. By the time we got there, we were all smiling and ready to have a wonderful, happy day together. And so we did.

We could have let Ricochet's impulsivity ruin our holiday. We could have thrown understanding and empathy out the window and held a grudge all day. We could have let ADHD ruin our Christmas. But instead, we overlooked what we can't change and made the most of it.

Where's our tailwind?

There was no disappointment in my special brand of parenthood quite like the squashed hopes of watching my child's ADHD medication turn his life around, then suddenly fail. The knot in the pit of my stomach when I saw it coming the second, third, fourth time it happened. Each time I became better at predicting it, but it somehow delivered a stronger punch, a bigger kick in the teeth to my emotions, energy level, and psyche. I knew this wasn't the worst blow a momma could face, but there isn't anything quite like seeing your child finally successful and happy, and then watch helplessly as they fall right back into the tight hold of struggling in nearly an instant.

The management of Ricochet's ADHD was constantly changing — success was a moving target. I stalked ADHD forums online, and read of kids who had been successfully on the same ADHD medicine for two or three years, maybe changing the dose once. I read of kids who were having great success with the first medication they tried, and I was jealous. The "why me" monster visited again. Why not us? Why couldn't we find the right medication regimen for Ricochet? Why couldn't we reach the maintenance portion of ADHD treatment?

It had been one year and one-and-a-half months since Ricochet began ADHD medication, and we were still constantly changing course. He was like a ship in the middle of the ocean, thrashing around aimlessly without the ability to gain control of its course — we were still searching for the tailwind to carry him smoothly in the right direction. I desperately wanted the wind in our sails to coast along for a while, for me and for Ricochet.

At the next counseling appointment, the therapist began by asking how things were going, as she always did.

"He's wasting away," I exclaimed. We immediately headed down the hall to weigh. He had lost four pounds in six weeks since increasing his dosage of Medication #3 for the third or fourth time. He was only forty-eight pounds then, at seven years old. Being five to ten pounds under average weight was a serious concern.

We went back into her office and talked in more detail about how everything was going. She noticed right away that Ricochet looked tired and down. I explained that he always looked that way since increasing the dose of Medication #3 again. When it was first increased, I was constantly asking him what was wrong and if he was sleepy. His answer was always that he was fine, nothing was wrong. Mr. T and I wondered if the dose was too high for him, but we hung tight to give it a chance. With the weight loss, the sleepy-sad look, and the rebound in the evenings we hadn't experienced on smaller doses of Medication #3, we suspected the higher dose wasn't going to be the answer to Ricochet's medication woes, either.

The therapist grabbed Ricochet's chart, and went speak to the behavioral pediatrician about what was happening with Ricochet on the higher dose. We had an appointment with him a week later, so I planned to wait until then to discuss the medication. She wasn't at all happy with what she was seeing, and decided it had to be addressed right then. I certainly didn't object. The pediatrician pored over Ricochet's chart, studying the spreadsheet I provided that chronicled the medication trials Ricochet endured before switching over to his care. He came in to the therapist's office about ten minutes later with a new plan. He decided to try Non-Stimulant #2, a long-acting version of the blood pressure medication Ricochet had taken with his stimulant a few months before. We were to slowly increase the dose while tapering down on Medication #3, so we could get to a point where he'd have just Non-Stimulant #2 for a week or so before our next appointment. That way, we could see if Non-Stimulant #2 alone would work for Ricochet. The behavioral pediatrician suspected we'd end up with a mild dose of Non-Stimulant #2 and a mild dose of Medication #3 together, but it was a process to get there.

I had an open mind and, as always, way too much hope riding on this new medication plan.

The first day was good — really good. The second day, he had a couple of bouts of extreme emotion, but I expected that when he was getting used to a new medication. On the third morning, I had to wake him for school. I hadn't had to wake him but two or three times that year because he was usually up thirty to forty-five minutes before anyone else. He was in no mood to be woken that morning though, and refused to dress and go to school. That was new behavior, with or without medication, and I did not like it. We barely made it to school on time.

I decided to try a different approach to gather feedback on this medication change, and I didn't tell anyone outside our household about the change. I wanted to see what differences others noticed without tipping them off that there had been a change. I planned to tell his teacher in our conference a few days later, if she didn't notice beforehand. I wanted to know that the changes were bold enough to be obvious.

I weaned Ricochet off Medication #3 and slowly increased the dosage of Non-Stimulant #2, as instructed. He was on the minimum of Non-Stimulant #2 only one day because it obviously wasn't going to work — he was out of control, tattooing himself up his legs with ink pens during school, and showing a severe lack of respect. I bumped him up to 2 mg of Non-Stimulant #2 the second day off Medication #3, but that was worse. He sat in school and drew pictures of himself crying instead of doing his work. He back-talked his teacher, which had never happened before. He refused anything and everything he was asked to do.

We had therapy again that afternoon.

"How are things going?" the therapist asked.

"The new medicine is not helping, not one bit. I have lots of bad behavior," Ricochet said. That entire day was heartbreaking, even for him. Even Ricochet knew he was out of control, and he was very unhappy about it.

I made the decision to go ahead and add back in the moderate dose of Medication #3 the next morning. As we were tapering off it, I had noticed the moderate dose of Medication #3 with the starter dose of Non-Stimulant #2 seemed to work pretty well. I called the behavioral pediatrician to confirm that was okay, and I received his approval.

Ricochet had a medication check-up again five days after this new combination. I thought through those last several days to form a conclusion about the efficacy of this cocktail of ADHD medications, and decided it was working pretty well. I had increased Non-Stimulant #2 as instructed a couple of days prior, and I was a little concerned that the higher dose was a bit too much in combination with Medication #3, but I knew it hadn't been long enough to really decide that yet. No sooner had Ricochet and I discussed how we both felt the current medications and the combination were working well, than we entered the doctor's office and his behavior fell apart. He was mean to me and down on himself. He went from being happy and kind of carefree one minute, to being angry the next, to upset with himself and his feelings after that. We hadn't experienced this outside of taking medication, ever, but we had seen it with medications he couldn't tolerate.

I planned to give it another day or two just to be sure, but if those erratic mood shifts continued, I would request that Non-Stimulant #2 be decreased to the lower dose. I still had no tolerance for medications that made my sweet little boy's behavior and temperament worse.

The price of chaos

It was another typical school morning in the Williams household. Ricochet was up before anyone else, playing Lego Star Wars on the Wii and stuffing Mr. T's Oreos in his mouth as fast as he could. Warrior Girl gave me lip every time I asked her to do something.

Since Ricochet had binged on sweets this morning, a sure way to increase hyperactivity and mood issues, he was particularly indignant and defiant. I had to constantly ask for him to attempt to take care of dressing, eating, and swallowing his pills. On non-sugar mornings, he was pretty cooperative, but still needed constant supervision to be sure he was on task and ready on time. On sugar-filled mornings, all bets were off.

This sugar-high morning was mixed with a particularly escalated tween-queen attitude. And then there was Mr. T — he wasn't good with mornings, either. Usually, he was up and out the door for work before anyone else woke each weekday, but his boss had just implemented massive lay-offs and switched remaining employees to a four-day work week. So Mr. T was home this Friday morning and as grumpy as ever. When I asked him where he was going because he was up early on his day off, he had an "I'm too tired to answer to anyone, even my wife, especially my wife" reaction, and snapped at me.

So Warrior Girl was giving me lip, Ricochet drained all my energy, Mr. T just snapped at me and evaded my question, and I was trying to leave early to get Warrior Girl to school and Ricochet to counseling on time. Imagine all the thoughts bumping around in my head. Imagine the conversation I'm having with Ricochet about the brand new packs of markers and colored pencils he snuck into his backpack before I was ready for him to take yet another set to school, never to see them again.

Imagine that conversation and the chaos in my head as I backed out of the garage that Friday morning.

<<<CRASH!!!!!>>>

{GASP!}

My head dropped. My hands rose to meet it. Reality played in slow motion.

I t-boned my own husband's parked car backing out of the garage in my own driveway!

WHAT?

I cried as I called Mr. T to come outside and see what I'd done. I cried all the way to school, despite Mr. T being very, very cool about it. I cried almost all the way to the counselor's office, too. Every time I thought I had myself together, one little thought of the caved-in passenger door of Mr. T's car, a mistake we didn't have the funds to fix, sent me right back over the edge.

I am very intelligent, organized, and 100% guided by common sense. This incident was not me. I didn't do irresponsible things. Sure, I made mistakes, but not like this. I was dreadfully embarrassed.

In hindsight, I can say "of course this happened." Of course something so bloody stupid is born of so much chaos and a blind state of overwhelm. This was par for the course in my special brand of parenthood.

Corralling homework

Homework is a B#%@*. For a kid with ADHD, it's downright cruel, if you ask me. I struggled for two years to create a plan for homework that would incite the least resistance, arguments, and tears. I started by playing around with the time of day homework was completed in order to determine the time Ricochet could be most successful. Then, I enforced a consistent homework schedule. I first tried homework right after school, thinking medication would still be effective and that we should simply get it over with. That was a disaster. He needed free time to unwind after being in school for seven hours, forced to comply with someone else's plans. He usually watched TV or played computer games and ate a snack right after arriving home.

We also tried after dinner, when the school day was a distant memory. That time wasn't the battle to get Ricochet to agree to do homework that immediately after school was. However, his medication was no longer helping him slow down, and the battle presented in actually getting anything accomplished. Four o'clock turned out to be our "magic" homework hour. Now, I use the term "magic" very loosely. My son will never be willing to do homework, nor will he be efficient at it. Finding what worked best under our circumstances was the magic for our family. It may not be magic for a typically-abled child, but it's magic in our house.

At 4 PM, about an hour after arriving home from school, all electronics were turned off and Ricochet and I sat down at the dining room table for homework. We had a busy therapy and extracurricular schedule, so we sometimes started homework early at 3:30 PM if we were going to have to head out the door around our regular homework time. Some days, we were too busy and skipped it altogether, which was okay with Ricochet's teacher. Ms. Glinda believed that evenings are family time and shouldn't be filled with the stress of homework.

Her expectation was that they learn their spelling words by Friday morning and do some reading. Since Ricochet had such a phenomenal memory, we could get away with learning spelling words two or three nights a week, instead of four. Plus, their school day was 50% reading, so I didn't force him to read with me every afternoon for homework. He had a flashlight in bed and read to himself a few nights a week before falling asleep anyway. I decided to wait until third grade the next year, when homework requirements would increase greatly, to be so stressed out every evening.

We started homework each afternoon with spelling words. Ricochet used special paper with boxes for each letter to help with legibility. He refused to use this different paper at school in front of his peers, but he used it at home successfully. It made an astonishing difference in the legibility of his handwriting because he was forced to slow down tremendously to put each letter in its own box. I let Ricochet pick out the pencil he wanted to use. His occupational therapist suggested he use golf pencils, #2 pencils that are really short and require you to hold them closer to the lead, and he often chose them.

Ten minutes into homework, Ricochet had gathered the writing utensil of his choice and his special paper, but he was still grumbling about doing homework. "I don't want to do spelling," he would say in a babyish whine. Even the best laid plan would not cure resistance to homework. I hoped when he was older he'd have the compensation tools to know it's hard but it has to be done. At this point, I accepted that he'd continue to complain about homework. However, we reached a point where the complaining was only the first few minutes with structure and consistency. Once he realized he could do something successfully and receive praise for it, he stopped complaining.

Praise was crucial and part of our homework ground rules as well. I praised him over and over for every little accomplishment to continue momentum through to completion. For instance, I quizzed Ricochet on his spelling words each homework period, but quizzed him only on the words he missed the day before. That meant spelling homework got shorter and shorter each day. I watched him spell the words and made a huge deal every time he got one right. He was excited to move on to the next word when he had just nailed one. Then we reviewed how to remember the spelling of the words he missed, and he wrote each one correctly one time. Yes, he wanted to quit each and every time he misspelled a word, but at least it wasn't every moment of the entire task. I drew smiley faces beside correct words, and he eventually did that himself.

Ricochet's 504 Plan included an accommodation that he could finish incomplete classwork at home. Once or twice a week, he had a writing assignment or a math worksheet in addition to the spelling. Math was never a problem — it was his talent, and he loved to do it because it made him feel capable. The writing was a huge challenge though, and definitely his biggest struggle. I tried to save writing assignments for an afternoon when homework was going well and his demeanor was good, or for the weekend when there was no other "work" except that.

Through trial and error, we found what worked for Ricochet and me with this particular teacher. The next school year we would go through the same experiment all over again, but I was beginning to learn how to help Ricochet.

6
Peeling back the onion

"Everybody is a genius. But if you judge a fish by its ability to climb a tree, it will live its whole life believing that it is stupid."
— *Albert Einstein*

Realizing it was more than ADHD

It's hard for me to understand anyone having difficulty writing. I am a writer, after all. Just put pen to paper, fingertips to keyboard, and go with whatever comes out. You can always edit your thoughts later and polish for something cohesive. That's how I do it anyway.

I learned it's not always that easy for some. Ricochet already had a well-documented difficulty with handwriting, as many individuals with ADHD do. I felt like he struggled with the process of writing, or written expression, because he found handwriting so difficult. This was common sense: avoid anything that requires handwriting when it's so hard.

In second grade, though, I began to realize that his problem with writing was much more than a difficulty forming letters with pencil to paper. Most of the work Ricochet was bringing home incomplete to finish was his writing assignment. Ms. Glinda worked closely with him at school, and he was supposed to get the second grade aide's personal attention during writing as soon as they could rework her schedule. But he was still struggling greatly.

One day, Ms. Glinda sent home what she was able to finish with him of that day's short story assignment and asked that I help him complete it. He took out a page in her handwriting with the story starter, "My trip to the beach," and a list of phrases about the subject:

- saw crabs
- collected shells
- went boogie boarding
- climbed the lighthouse
- etc...

He had at least a dozen phrases in all, and they described our camping trip the previous summer. I thought it would be easy to complete the assignment because he already described the trip and simply had to put these thoughts into sentences. Boy, was I wrong! It was a major battle to simply get started.

"I don't know what to say. I don't know which ones to choose. I can't do it. It's too hard," Ricochet whined.

I was a little too hard on him at first, thinking he simply didn't want to do it. I couldn't understand how he could have this list of phrases in front of him and not be able to put together a short story. The further we got into it, the further I realized the thoughts were a jumbled mess in his mind. It wasn't laziness or stubbornness, but a real difficulty with planning and organization. I asked him to describe the trip to me, and he did so eloquently and with impressive vocabulary. When I asked him to write it down immediately after speaking it to me, he couldn't begin to. This was very alarming!

As usual, I sat down at the computer and began Internet research to try to solve my kiddo's problem. I found that expressive writing difficulty is part of the inadequate executive functions in ADHD: taking an issue apart, analyzing the pieces, reconstituting, and organizing it into new ideas (complex problem solving).

A research study by Mayes and Calhoun identified written expression as the most common learning problem among students with ADHD. Consequently, writing essays, drafting book reports, and answering open questions on tests or homework is often very challenging for students with ADHD. For example, when writing essays, students often have difficulty: holding ideas in mind; acting upon and organizing ideas; quickly retrieving grammar, spelling, and punctuation rules from long-term memory; manipulating all this information; remembering ideas to write down; organizing the material in a logical sequence; and then reviewing and correcting errors.[5]

Written Expression Disorder encompasses handwriting complications as well as disorganization of thoughts, while Dysgraphia involves problems with handwriting, spelling, and forming ideas. Ricochet struggles with two out of three, but did well with spelling (his memory was off the charts).

The descriptions of Written Expression Disorder and Dysgraphia both fit Ricochet, yet I couldn't find concrete suggestions on how to help a child with these learning disabilities. Most of the suggestions were accommodations we'd already tried with little or no success.

After this revelation that Ricochet was also struggling with written expression, I emailed the 504 Plan manager to see what accommodations we could add to help Ricochet with writing, now that I determined it was a much bigger dysfunction than I initially thought. This time I didn't know what to do and didn't have a plan.

We thought ADHD was Ricochet's only diagnosis at first — he was wild and distracted, but super smart and super sweet. His handwriting was notably atrocious, but who cares? Maybe he'd become a doctor, right? As time passed, other differences continued to reveal themselves. His altered sensory responses became more apparent the more knowledgeable I became about sensory integration and Sensory Processing Disorder (SPD). I saw anxiety rear its ugly head very often during the school year, too. I had now peeled back the layers of Ricochet's neurobiology to uncover more concerns, not merely ADHD.

Sensory issues and anxiety were difficult at times, but I found them manageable. A learning disability was another animal, though. You can't learn skills or take medication for it, you can only construct a life that compensates. Handling learning disabilities is much more complex and difficult than ADHD. In all these hours reading and researching learning disabilities, I still couldn't figure out how to help my son. A writing disorder is pervasive and affects all academics. Not only does his learning disability make success in the subject of writing nearly impossible, it also inhibited his performance in math, social studies, and science, all subjects he would normally excel in. Worst of all, it made him feel "stupid," making for one sad momma.

After many months with ADHD medications, new learning disabilities, and new diagnoses, we were still constantly changing course. I was still searching for the tailwind to carry us in the right direction.

Noticing the gap

Ricochet and his cousin, Creative H, were very close when they were young. We shared a house for a while when Creative H was born, barely a year after Ricochet, and then the kids stayed in the care of Grandma most days while my sister and I worked. Up until Ricochet started kindergarten, they were like brother and sister.

When Creative H started school, they had just moved to a new house on the other side of town, and Ricochet and Creative H didn't get to spend much time together, so we invited Creative H for a sleepover. Ricochet was thrilled. Creative H was thrilled. There was great anticipation.

As time went on, I noticed Creative H became aware of the differences between her and Ricochet. She asked if he was sick: "Is that why he takes medicine every day?" Not knowing how to explain ADHD to a six-year-old other than pointing out his differences, I paused and my sister jumped in and told her it is just like her daddy taking vitamins every day. *Good enough for that time*, I thought.

Creative H was noticing more than just the daily medication, though. She seemed to study Ricochet when he was hyper or when he couldn't quite come to grips with change. She couldn't understand why he was so obsessed with Lego Star Wars, computer games, and his Nintendo.

She quizzed me when she awoke the next morning. "Why doesn't Ricochet want to play anything but Lego Star Wars?" She is very smart and observant and was noticing his differences.

"He just really likes Lego Star Wars, sweetie. Sometimes his brain gets stuck on something he likes for a long time."

It didn't bother me that she questioned his differences; some day she would notice his talents, too.

Creative H was quick to ask to sleep somewhere other than with Ricochet when she realized he was too excited to be still and go to sleep, but the sleepover was otherwise a raving success. In the morning they sang and danced together, and the sound of their laughter and joy, their sameness, filled our house.

A typical morning

By early spring of Ricochet's second grade year, a year and a half after diagnosis, many more days were finally becoming predictable — our sort of predictable anyway, where nothing out of the ordinary occurs, good or bad.

It was usually a struggle to get Ricochet dressed and ready for school. Some days it was so easy I wondered what was going on with him. Other days, such as the days he got into the cookies before anyone else awoke, I thought I might run out of the house screaming and not look back before he'd ever be ready to go. But most days by this point were simply typical.

The alarm clock sounded at 6 AM. The first alarm was for Mr. T, but I managed the alarm clock or he'd never get up. I nudged him. "It's six," I warned. A faint groan was progress. I already hit the snooze because I knew he wouldn't actually get up then. This was just the pre-alarm to start the thirty to fifty-minute waking process. The alarm sounded every ten minutes. I continued to relay the time every ten minutes. Eventually, he got moving and was out the door in a flash (if only we could all go to work in a baseball cap and torn jeans).

So I was awake — conscious, but not yet moving — when Ricochet got up, mere moments after the first alarm. He turned on the hall light, illuminating the entryway to our bedroom, and headed straight downstairs. Some mornings, the television went on right away and the vibration came straight up into our bedroom. Those were loud mornings. Some mornings, he got his Nintendo and curled up on the sofa under a blanket. He was quiet and peaceful. These mornings, I would lie in bed a bit longer because I knew he was not eating cookies and using the furniture for a make-shift trampoline. I preferred these mornings.

I lay in bed a little too long this particular spring morning, so I called down to Ricochet to come up and get dressed, rather than going down and checking things out first. The quiet tricked me into thinking he might actually be calm and compliant.

"No! I'm NOT coming. I'm NOT going to get dressed!" he shouted to be certain his words would reach me upstairs.

"Ricochet, it's time to get dressed for school. Are you going to come upstairs, or do I have to start my count?"

"No! I don't want to get dressed!" he said with a twangier whine.

"I have to start my count then. I would hate for you to lose your screen time today like you did yesterday."

"No, don't count. I don't want to come up."

"Okay. That's three…"

"No!"

"Two…"

"Fine! … Fine! I'm *coming*!!!"

I often resorted to this counting technique our counselor taught me, and it usually ended with that distinct "Fine!" before I got to "one" and a consequence. I wish I could convey the tone of his "Fine!" here on this page. It was this "You won. I can't believe you won. I can't believe I can't make any of my own decisions. I'm so very disturbed that you won again," sort of tone. The way he said it was so humorous. Mr. T and I couldn't help but laugh when it emerged, and it came many times a day then. We honestly had to turn our heads and hold in a chuckle.

Once he realized he wasn't winning, Ricochet stomped upstairs. I had his clothes out and toothpaste on his toothbrush. He brushed his teeth first, without incident. He then came into his room and proceeded to tell me I didn't give him underwear. Of course I did. It was right on top of the stack of clothes. He laughed and

Here's the compliance technique Ricochet's counselor taught us:

State very simply and calmly what you want the child to do (i.e., "I need you to come upstairs and get dressed now.")

If the child doesn't comply, state, "I'm going to start my count now." Then wait five full seconds for a reaction. (Many kids with ADHD have very slow processing. This five-second lag made all the difference in the world — counting finally worked to initiate compliance when it had never worked before.)

Still no compliance? State very calmly, "That's one." Remember, once the count is started, there's no negotiation and no repeating the task; just count.

Wait five seconds again.

Still no compliance? "That's two." Do not escalate the tone or volume of your voice. Remain stern and serious, but calm and not angry.

If the child still doesn't comply after another five seconds. "That's three. You now {insert your consequence here}." (I always allow opportunities to earn it back with exemplary behavior.)

It's important to define the consequence before starting the count. I always use the same consequence (loss of screen time) because that is the most motivating for Ricochet, and I don't want to enter a negotiation for consequences each time.

tried to convince me that I didn't, and it escalated into an annoying game of procrastination.

"Do you want me to start my count again?" I asked.

His clothes started going on his body. It looked like he was going to get it done, so I went downstairs to make the kids some breakfast before we had to run out the door.

Ricochet came downstairs five minutes later with his underwear, pants, and even socks on. But he still had his pajama shirt on. And he was wearing a huge, Cheshire Cat sort of grin on his face.

"Go back up and get your shirt on, please."

"Fine!" he hollered.

At least there was no argument that time. I wouldn't tell him, but I would've let him go in the pajama shirt if I had to. I tried to keep him from getting picked on, and the shirt was obviously pajamas, but I had learned to pick my battles.

He came back quickly, appropriately dressed, and sat down at the snack bar for breakfast. By then I had his instant breakfast (I added it to his milk to boost calories), two pills, and a donut ready for him. What was I thinking giving this hyperactive kid donuts! Mr. T had a thing for donuts and had brought a box home the day before. It was hard to tell the kids certain things were okay for their daddy, but not for them. I was all the time lecturing them about eating real, natural food instead of processed, fake, junk foods, but Mr. T likes to eat crap (*sorry, Mr. T*), and so it was in the house.

I had to ask him a few times to finish his milk. He never drank it all. I actually followed him around and put the straw up to his mouth for sips (although I encouraged gulps). That sounds pathetic, but he didn't get enough to eat between the loss of appetite medication side effect and the distraction factor that had him leaving his food before he was really full. I made him stay at the dinner table until everyone was finished eating or he had cleared his plate. If I made him stay, he always ate more. He whined about doing something else, but he ate more. And then he gorged at 8 PM most nights, just before going to bed.

So Ricochet was dressed. He ate breakfast. He brushed his teeth. He took his pills. He was rummaging through the sofa looking for something he lost.

"Time to get your shoes on. Come over here, and I'll help you get your tie-shoes on."

"I don't want to wear those."

"That's all you have to wear now that there's a giant hole in the bottom of the others."

"I don't care about the hole."

"I do. I want your feet to be safe. Shoes can't protect your feet with a hole in the bottom."

He walked over to the shoe cubby, and pulled out his snow boots. "I'll wear these then."

"It's going to be sixty-something degrees today. You cannot wear snow boots."

I pulled out his new Converse tie shoes. "Let's get these on. I'll help you."

He actually let me put them on him without further struggle. Before I could get my own shoes and jacket, much less find my cell phone and keys, he had his jacket and backpack on and was standing by the door.

Ahhh... I made it without raising my voice today.

7
Simply Trying to Get Through Each Day, Again

"Study strategy over the years and achieve the spirit of the warrior. Today is victory over yourself of yesterday; tomorrow is your victory over lesser men."
— *Miyamoto Musashi*

I'm a moron

Ricochet called me a "moron" several times one morning while trying to get ready for school. Not in a roundabout way, not as a joke. Just flat out, "You're a moron, Mom!" I could tell he was serious because he called me sterile old "Mom" instead of his usual "Momma."

"If you don't get upstairs and get your clothes on for school, I'll take away your screen time today," I said calmly. This was at least the third time I'd asked him already.

"You're a moron, Mom!"

I removed the lingering cookie from the previous evening's dessert from his hands. "You cannot have cookies for breakfast, but you can have them when you get home from school."

"You're a moron, Mom!"

"It is time to get your shoes on. We have to leave for school soon. I've asked you three times, and now you must get your shoes on."

"You're a moron, Mom!"

"Get your backpack and get in the car before I completely lose it with you, Ricochet."

"You're a moron!" he screamed one last time, and his echo repeated as he descended the stairs to the garage.

I am not unintelligent. In fact, we two gifted parents made two gifted children. I am not gullible (usually). I am not oblivious to the ways of the world. I am a very intelligent gal. Yet, he called me a moron... over and over and over again.

Even more disturbing than the name calling and disrespect was that my sweet little boy had never once called me a moron before he started ADHD medication. That had me asking, *Could I really be a moron?*

Could I have actually been dumb enough, excuse me, moronic enough to think medication for ADHD would be foolproof? That somehow giving him medication after asking him to get dressed and ready for school would work out well? That leaving his half-eaten cookie right on the kitchen counter would not result in him wanting to eat it the next morning? That pushing and yelling for compliance wouldn't escalate into a battle of wills? That medication wouldn't somehow alter him even during periods when it had "worn off"? Okay, I concede on that one. I *did* think he would just be the same sweet, mischievous Ricochet from before his ADHD diagnosis when the medication wasn't in effect. This alter-ego, between-doses kid I could do without.

This behavior was a clear signal for me — this was the pit we always fell into when Ricochet's medications failed. His behaviors escalated and my hopes for successful treatment plummeted.

A tidal wave of sorry

Sorry was a big part of my life parenting a child with ADHD.

- I was sorry when I lost my patience over behaviors Ricochet couldn't help.
- I was sorry when people stared because he was jumping around as if he *literally* had ants in his pants while simply walking through the grocery store.
- I was sorry when kids decided not to play with him because his activity level overwhelmed them.
- I was sorry when people didn't understand him.
- I was sorry because I felt like I must have done something wrong to cause his ADHD.
- I was sorry when plans changed unexpectedly and threw him for a loop.
- I was sorry I couldn't send him to a school with an experiential learning philosophy.
- I was sorry... for so many things.

Now we could add a new sorry — feeling sorry *for* him. I guess this feeling wasn't really new. Before Ricochet was diagnosed, he was sad all the time and felt he couldn't please anyone, even himself. I certainly felt sorry for him then, every day. This new sorry felt somehow different. I think it was because, in trying to help him, Mr. T and I were creating unfortunate situations that caused us to feel sorry for Ricochet. This really hit hard on one of our beach vacations.

Ricochet switched medications (now on Medication #5) four days before we left home to spend spring break at the coast. The day before our trip, our counselor noticed his newest medicine wasn't working.

"I feel like it's actually exacerbating his ADHD symptoms, but I'm trying to give it adequate time to make a fair determination of its efficacy," I explained to her.

"There's no need to wait and see — we're seeing very clearly it isn't going to work in its current dose," she rebutted.

She spoke to the doctor, and he advised us to give Ricochet a second extended-release medication at 2 PM each day. Ricochet was already struggling a bit more with falling asleep at night on the morning dose, so I was leery of this new plan. The day we were to make our six-hour drive to the beach after Mr. T got home from work, the day after meeting with the counselor, I decided to try the short-acting formulation of the medication the doctor had prescribed originally. Ricochet would take it in the afternoon to extend the medication, instead of another extended-release. I gave him the lowest dose of this short-acting tablet at 2 PM.

Then all hell broke loose.

Ricochet couldn't contain himself on this short-acting medicine. As our counselor had said so appropriately the day before, "The medication hijacked his brain." He was literally bouncing off everything, climbing the walls, talking a mile a minute, and going so fast it seemed like he couldn't possibly keep up with himself. He was very clearly not in control.

The road trip to the beach was miserable for everyone. Ricochet was able to stay in his seat since he was buckled (my car doesn't move unless everyone is buckled), but he was loud and his arms and legs were flailing the entire drive. That was tolerable, but the jumping on the furniture and yelling in the condo until 3 AM was not — this was not our condo and we feared disturbing the neighbors. It was so *not* tolerable. Yet there was no choice. He wasn't in control of his body or mind at that point. Mr. T and I pleaded with him. We tried reasoning with him. We lay in his bed to cuddle him, but he couldn't lie with us. We tried rubbing his back to relax him, but it was hard to rub a moving target. Of course, we got frustrated. "Why can't you just..." became a routine phrase that poured off our lips that night. He was literally out of his mind.

Mr. T came out of the bedroom at one point, at least the third time he had tried to help Ricochet, and he lay down next to him. I was about to lose it completely by then.

"It doesn't matter what you do, Ricochet is not in control. We're just going to have to ride it out," I explained with conviction.

Mr. T looked over at me, and said, "I just feel so sorry for him."

It takes a lot for Mr. T to get past frustration, past the "Why can't you just..." and past the punishments and consequences, to just feeling sorry for Ricochet.

The most regrettable part of the situation was that we did that to him. I gave him the medicine that caused him to lose any and all self-control for thirteen hours (*uh, short-acting?*)! No, I couldn't have known. I knew that in my mind... but it didn't make my heart feel any better. I already carried a load of guilt that he even had ADHD, now I had to add a whole new bag of guilt for experimenting on him with ADHD medications. Helpful intentions or not, it still hurt. It hurt a lot.

Fortunately, by then I had been through enough medication trials with Ricochet to make a contingency plan before leaving home for a week. Realizing the new medication was not going well already, I packed the rest of the previous medicine he had not finished, Medication #3. The next morning, Ricochet had the previous medication again, and all was well. Our family enjoyed our time at the beach from then on.

Ricochet ended up having such a great time that week that he was sad when we returned home.

"I miss South Carolina, Momma. I miss the beach. I want to go back."

We always had the best time at the beach, especially Ricochet — nature was his only boundary.

When I needed him to be a quitter

It was just Ricochet and me at his baseball game one cold, rainy spring night. Mr. T and Warrior Girl had a softball game at a different field. I sat in the cold, trying to keep my umbrella from lifting inside-out and pulling me into flight, watching Ricochet's teammates play baseball. I sat shivering and miserable, and my kid only stepped on the field twice in a full six innings — once to bat (strike out) and once to play (around in) the outfield. What exactly was the point? I thought I must have been missing it.

Was it wrong to wish my child would quit something? I know it was human, but was it wrong? Was it wrong for me to want Ricochet to quit baseball because he spent the majority of every game on the bench? Probably... but that didn't stop me.

He wanted to be there, mind you. He wanted to play baseball, even though he didn't actually get to play much. Ricochet wanted to continue, despite not having any success, but I wanted him to quit because of his lack of success. It was exhausting to feel sorry for him every moment of every two-hour game. It was so tiring to make excuses for his behavior or the fact that he didn't want to actually go on the field and play the game. It was heartbreaking to see him and our family ostracized by the coaches and other parents. Ricochet was all but ignored, seen as an inconvenience rather than a child to nurture and teach a love of baseball.

I tried to reason with Ricochet all the way home that night — I tried to convince him to quit baseball. I felt just awful about it. But honestly, I felt more awful that he refused!

"Baseball is obviously not the best sport for you," I started. "Let's trade baseball for another activity, anything you want to try."

"No, Momma. I'm not a quitter." His reply was resolute.

"What about Taekwondo? You really want to do that, and I'll find the funds so you can if you quit baseball. Buddy, you don't even really play. You mostly sit in the dugout," I reasoned. "Something else will be more fun for you."

"No, I'm not a quitter. I'm not quitting. I like baseball."

There was no reasoning with him. He simply didn't perceive a problem. He didn't realize sitting the bench in baseball was a blaring message that you weren't as good as everyone else (except the other poor kid with matched hyperactivity who always sat the bench with Ricochet). He didn't realize all the other kids were looking at him differently and judging him. He didn't see his differences, and I should have been grateful for that.

Instead, I was disappointed. I wanted him on the field to learn the game and participate. I didn't want to drive all over town two or three times a week to watch other people's kids play baseball for nearly two hours. I wanted to watch my own child play and have fun, or I wanted to do something else with my time.

I was making every accommodation so Ricochet could play baseball, because he wanted to. I spoke to his coaches about his challenges. I asked the doctor to give him a short-acting medicine for the evenings he had baseball. I talked Ricochet through a plan — what to do when he was batting, and paying attention to the ball when he was in the outfield. I talked all the way to and from each game about these things. I tried everything I could think of, and I was still failing him. He was still sitting the bench. Baseball simply wasn't suited for him, but I struggled to convince Ricochet.

I went along with baseball as long as Ricochet wanted to play. An hour before his next game, he decided not to participate anymore. Yes, he quit baseball. As much as I had wanted him to quit sooner, I was glad it was his decision. It helped him learn how to decide if an activity is right for his differences.

Don't destroy your boat

Relationships with significant others are tough, even under the best circumstances. Throw some children and a highly-misunderstood behavioral disability in the mix, and they become exponentially tougher. When Ricochet was first diagnosed, Mr. T and I leaned on each other for support. We discussed all decisions about his ADHD treatment. It was tough, but we were in it together.

I had been obsessed with ADHD since Ricochet's diagnosis. I surrounded myself with ADHD books, websites, online forums, videos, etc. I was compelled to learn all I could until I had answers for my son. I spent many, many hours a day researching ADHD and an hour or two most days writing about it. Every night at dinner, I hurled ADHD facts and stories all over everyone. Mr. T came home from a long, hard day at work, sat down to eat dinner with his family, and listened to a diatribe about ADHD.

My obsession with ADHD was ruling my days completely. I awoke thinking about how ADHD was going to make it hard to get Ricochet ready for school. I thought about what he should eat for breakfast to get the most protein to help his brain focus. I watched him walk into the school building, and hoped ADHD didn't cause too many troubles for him that day. I came home to blog about ADHD, chat with other moms of kids with ADHD, and read, read, read all about ADHD.

I neglected housework to research. I might have taken a shower, but I was worrying about Ricochet at school as I lathered. I read books or magazines about ADHD as I sat in the car line, waiting for school to let out. I immediately asked Ricochet how his day was as he climbed into the car. I couldn't wait to get home and read the note his teacher sent about his day, hoping for little ADHD-related comments. I fought with Ricochet about homework because ADHD made it so hard. Then his medications would wear off, and it became all about trying to control his behaviors enough to keep everyone from madness and to keep him from destroying the house. Then it was time to beg him to eat dinner because his ADHD medication made him lose his appetite. Then we had to endure the bedtime battle, a battle only because of ADHD. The only time I was not completely absorbed in ADHD was 8-10 PM each night when the kids were in bed, and I vegetated in front of the television so I could stop thinking.

It took more than three years to realize I wasn't finding answers because I was asking the wrong questions. My burning questions, those that drove me to the point of obsession, didn't have answers.

Why MY son?

How do I fix his handwriting?

How do I keep him from getting in trouble at school?

How do I keep him from being bullied?
How do I keep him from failing?

I was driven to an insane thirst for all things ADHD because I wanted to "fix" it, but that was an impossibility.

My obsession silently wedged between Mr. T and me. I saw it coming in his blank stare when I told a story about the child of a "virtual" friend on my Facebook Fan Page, or beneath his belabored sigh when I explained the contents of yet another article on ADHD. I was pushing too hard.

While my obsession was maddening for Mr. T, I realized it wasn't healthy for me either. It was detrimental to everyone in our family, actually. Our lives couldn't be all about ADHD all the time — ADHD might feel all-consuming, but we couldn't permit it that power. In fact, our lives shouldn't be *about* ADHD at all. For example, say I have seasonal allergies. Does my life become all about allergies all the time? Of course not. I consider my allergy to all things blooming before taking a hike in the peak of spring, but I consider it, treat it, and then go on my hike. I wouldn't let allergies determine every facet of my life, and the same should be said for ADHD.

I knew my obsession had reached a breaking point when even I grew tired of reading, talking, and thinking about ADHD. I had given ADHD all the power in our family, and I had to make a genuine, concerted effort to regain control. I set a schedule to study and write about ADHD. I worked to think about something other than ADHD when I looked at Ricochet. I stopped feeling sorry for him, and once again focused on discovering and nurturing his gifts. I vowed not to discuss ADHD at the dinner table — if I had something ADHD-related to discuss with Mr. T, I would do it privately at a different time. I carved out some time to again focus on improving my real estate business. It took an enormous amount of self-awareness and effort, but ADHD no longer controlled my life.

Regaining control over the affect ADHD had on our family began to repair a broken portion of my marriage, too. There's a wonderful quote from a parent of a child with Fragile X Syndrome that illustrates this beautifully: "I tell couples who sail into a storm and are fighting: 'Don't hack at your boat in a storm. If you are in the middle of a crisis, don't take the very support you have and start whacking at it, because that is dumb. You should love, nurture, and care for the other person or you aren't going to make it through the storm.[6]'"

Mr. T and I had to stop going after each other over ADHD. Support was a casualty we couldn't afford.

8
Changing Expectations

*"The smallest act of kindness is worth more than
the grandest intentions."*
— *Oscar Wilde*

Clearly-defined expectations bring comfort

Kids want rules. As much as they contest it, it's true: they crave rules. They want to see their boundaries, whether they realize it or not. They need an eye on these lines both to stay within them to do the right thing, and to push them and overstep them when they feel like garnering (negative) attention or making a statement. Humans need to have clearly-defined expectations, and kids aren't immune to that.

I was anti-checklists/charts for quite some time. Those systems could be a lot to keep up with. I thought my disagreeable kids surely wouldn't comply with a written list every time they got ready for bed or ready for school. Still, I finally gave in to ADHD community pressure to create checklists and reward systems the second spring after Ricochet's diagnosis, and created morning and bedtime routine checklists for each of my children. I was desperate to find something, anything, to make mornings and bedtime easier to tolerate with Ricochet. Desperation drove me to checklists and, I must admit, I'm glad it did.

I started with the bedtime routine checklist. The kids treated it somewhat like a scavenger hunt, list in hand, moving from place to place, trying to earn the reward at the end. They each had a laminated checklist card and carried it around their bedrooms and the bathroom, completing each item. Each card had a large paperclip on the side pointing to a task, and they moved the clip to the next as they finished each task. The paperclip marked their place in the process and ensured they completed things in order.

This simple system worked like a charm. Bedtime was a breeze. Ricochet was still a little silly, but he finished everything and got into bed without arguing. I strutted like a proud peacock as I exited his room after tucking him in the first night he used the bedtime checklist.

As stoked as I was about the bedtime routine finally going well, I was certain mornings wouldn't be so simple. Mornings at that time were very, very bad — so bad, I wondered if there was any hope.

I didn't have much faith that the morning routine checklist had the power to bring positive changes to our early daily interactions. Everything is worth a try when you're dealing with something as unpredictable as ADHD, though. So give it a try we did, the very next morning. Ricochet seemed to enjoy the bedtime checklist the night before, so I woke him excitedly, and told him it was time to complete the morning routine checklist. I put as much excitement into it as I could while keeping it genuine.

I laid his clothes on the chair in his room, handed him the checklist, and told him I was going to get myself dressed. He agreed to work on the list for me while I got ready. It felt too good to be true, but we had plenty of time, so I was willing to walk away and give it a try. Once I was dressed and had brushed my teeth, I went to assess his progress. Much to my amazement he had put his clothes on, put his pj's in the hamper, brushed his teeth, and swished mouthwash. He was ready to go downstairs for breakfast. I was astonished — it was working beautifully.

He decided what he wanted for breakfast right away, and sat at the snack bar. He ate with pretty good focus while I packed his lunch. Then, he was able to move his clip to the final item:

If complete before 7:20 AM, you get to play a video game and earn 1 token.

It was 7:05 AM. He was excited and turned his game right on. I dropped a bonus token in his jar for doing such a great job and not refusing one item on his checklist. We got out of the house on time and happy, and no one yelled even once that morning. No power struggles. No refusing to complete necessary tasks. Nothing but sweet compliance and bright smiles. That was one for the record books.

I feared the novelty might wear off, but decided not to think about that. The system was going great, and I was determined to enjoy it.

Our simple system worked because the checklists provided the kids with consistent and clearly-defined expectations. The structure removed anxiety and provided room for calm. Imagine I am asked to stay within "my area." With an outline on the floor around me, I'd feel good that I could stay within that area — I'd know where the boundaries are, and I'd be comfortable with the task. But if I were asked to stay within "my area" and there were no visible boundaries, nor instructions to define the boundaries, I'd likely feel anxious about my ability to comply with this task. I'd be uncomfortable. The power of clearly-defined expectations is distinctly logical. Of course, adding a reward at the end further encourages successful completion of the task.

I couldn't assume Ricochet knew his boundaries for any given task. Yes, sometimes things are purely common sense, but common sense wasn't always present for a child with ADHD. I erred on the side of defining too much, rather than too little, and saw the benefits of clearly-defined expectations in our family.

The balance between disability and discipline

I felt expecting neurotypical behavior from Ricochet and punishing accordingly wasn't fair, because sometimes unwanted behaviors were out of his control due to his ADHD. Blaming ADHD for every behavior, saying, "He just can't help it," wouldn't teach him how to compensate and behave appropriately in the real world either. I was learning that defining expectations, along with consistent discipline, was paramount.

As a parent of a child with ADHD, I struggled immensely with discipline. It's ironic, since I had no problem being fair but firm in enforcing rules before Ricochet's diagnosis, and I still had no problem doling out punishment for his neurotypical big sister, either. Rationally, discipline is easy — every action has a reaction, so every bad choice has a bad reaction, or a consequence.

When ADHD is thrown into the mix, fairness in consequences is a foreign ideal. What is a fair consequence to a child whose brain typically prevents weighing consequences before taking action? Is the answer to skip consequences altogether when a child has ADHD?

That is what I did for some time, at first. I allowed Ricochet to use ADHD as a crutch, an excuse for bad decisions and undesirable behavior. I wasn't merely allowing it, I was *teaching* it. My response each time someone punished him was, "You have to remember, he can't help it."

I blogged one day about feeling bad when Ricochet was punished for behaviors related to his ADHD — behaviors that weren't acceptable normally, but which he couldn't help. I received some harsh feedback in the way of reader comments that pushed me to a startling realization — that attitude was doing Ricochet more harm than good.

One of my blog readers wrote:

Insisting that Ricochet has no control over his behavior teaches him that ADHD is a good excuse for misbehaving. This is, in essence, telling Ricochet that he can choose to not make the effort to control his behaviors. Ricochet will not be allowed to tell his boss someday that the reason he didn't accomplish the required tasks is that he has ADHD. To me, ADHD means that he has trouble controlling his actions, words, and impulses. It does not mean that it's impossible for him to control himself, nor does it mean that it is impossible for him to learn to control himself.

I still struggle with defining appropriate behaviors for my daughter, and I know a lot of you do too. It certainly isn't okay to expect perfect neurotypical behavior. It also isn't okay to teach them to use ADHD as an excuse to never learn appropriate social and life skills and to never be accountable for their actions.

Ouch! It hurt to be so clearly proven wrong, but it was the kick-in-the-pants I needed.

It was easier for me to discipline, and easier for Ricochet to act appropriately and not need discipline, if expectations were clearly and repeatedly defined. That was job number one, and I was already on it. For example, before heading into a store, I talked to him about why we were there and that we would not be purchasing any toys or candy. It also helped to have his electronics to keep his mind busy so he didn't engage in the constant diatribe of 'I want that's.' Most times, he whined about it and still begged some, but he got over it before it deteriorated into a meltdown. Other times, no amount of preparation would avoid such an event.

Consistency in discipline was the other key ingredient, and we certainly didn't have that down yet. Not just my consistency, but consistency among all his caregivers, and that was difficult. Ricochet knew the consequences for negative behaviors we were targeting at a given time because I defined them at the outset.

It took some time, but I unraveled the mess I caused and taught Ricochet that ADHD is not an excuse to misbehave and break the rules. At times, I still find myself (or am reminded by Mr. T that I am) falling back into the trap of using ADHD as an excuse. Implementing an appropriate discipline balance, despite ADHD, was an ongoing parenting challenge, but one I was determined to conquer.

The power of a big squeeze

The occupational therapist Ricochet had been seeing twice a month throughout second grade taught me a most interesting and simple way to bring comfort and stop a disturbance before it deteriorated into a full-blown meltdown: a big, long squeeze. Yep, it could be as simple as a bear hug.

She frequently explained to me the reasons for his loud voice, exaggerated movements, or crashing into things. At this particular therapy appointment, she explained that children like Ricochet lack appropriate proprioceptive input, the sensory feedback that tells one about movement and body position. It is one of the deep senses and could be considered the "position sense" (as it's referred to in the book *The Out-of-Sync Child*). It's crucial for feeling grounded and knowing where you are in space. Children with proprioception difficulties need deep sensory input to feel grounded and aware of their bodies, so she gave me a list of recommended activities. While many of the activities on her list included carrying heavy objects or doing somewhat laborious physical exercise, one activity stood out from the rest — hugging. Big, giant, full-squeeze bear hugs provide the pressure that makes Ricochet feel secure, and can also be very calming. I soon realized that these bear hugs were a powerful tool to extinguish looming meltdowns as well.

I first tested the power of a big squeeze for Ricochet one Saturday night while at our local minor league baseball game. I knew a 7 PM game wasn't ideal for Ricochet, since his medicine wore off before then, and watching the entire game would mean being up at least two hours after bedtime. But it was much cooler at night, and it didn't hijack an entire day like a mid-afternoon game, so we went for it.

This particular Saturday also happened to be the first day Ricochet started Medicine #6, a change made toward the end of second grade, when we just couldn't get any dosage of Medication #3 quite right the third time around. New medication day isn't the best time for public activities, I know, but Ricochet was doing well, and we'd already done something else out of the norm that day without incident. He loved to go to these games, not to watch baseball, but for the opportunity to play with his cousin, Creative H.

Ricochet was excited to go to the ballgame that evening. We found our seats, and got the kids some dinner from concessions. We coasted along as usual for the first hour or so. Then Ricochet looked over at me out of the blue, and said, "How much longer? I want to go home."

"They just started the fourth inning. We aren't quite half-way through the game yet," I explained calmly, pointing at the score board so he'd have a visual.

His mood instantly spiraled, and the tone of his voice met a very high pitch. "I want to go home now! Right now! I'm not waiting." His eyes were squinted tight, his face red, his arms folded tightly across his chest.

At that moment, I could have argued with him. I could have told him he was doing what I said, or what the group wanted, but the situation only would have worsened. I knew he was on edge, and taking a hard line would escalate the situation.

Instead, I drew him in, folded his legs and arms to his chest, and squeezed. I felt his body release the tension after a few seconds, and he melted into me. As he lay there, head on my lap, I kept one arm around him tightly and massaged the back of his head with the other. He stayed there for about fifteen minutes. In the end, he was calm and went back to playing with Creative H. Because of his proprioceptive deficit, some measured sensory input was just what he needed to be soothed.

I reached the point in learning to effectively parent my child where I finally sensed when Ricochet was heading toward a meltdown, as I did at that ballgame. If implemented early, these bear hugs could calm him enough for redirection and often avoid a full meltdown.

There's no excuse

Ricochet enjoyed occupational therapy, an outlet for his unwavering energy, and I continued to enjoy the insights his therapists shared with me. One summer day between second and third grade, Ricochet was working on throwing and catching during therapy. When the OT gave me a recap after his session, I confirmed that Ricochet needed help with that very activity.

"We had a tough time with baseball this year," I said as I gave Ricochet a soothing pat on the back. "Didn't we, Buddy?"

His therapist answered with great conviction. "That's why we work on basic skills like throwing and catching; every one of these kids should be included in everything other children do. We need to teach them the necessary skills and make the appropriate accommodations so they can have childhood experiences like any other child."

This statement impacted me intensely. I often weighed what activities we should and shouldn't do with Ricochet based on his ADHD. I was definitely guilty of avoiding certain activities and particular public places because I knew my son would not respond like a neurotypical child. I probably wouldn't have taken Ricochet back to Little League after the first year if Mr. T and Warrior Girl had not been so involved. I consistently read that certain sports were better for an ADHD brain than others, but I knew for a fact there were professional baseball players with ADHD. If their families had said, "No, you aren't meant for baseball," they would have missed their passion and possibly life success.

Thanks to the occupational therapist's remarks, I realized it was important to offer Ricochet all the opportunities and experiences we would offer if he didn't have special needs. He needed to try what interested him and make up his own mind. My child with ADHD could be like other children. He could find ways to compensate for his differences to participate with success.

Ricochet was ultra-sensitive to loud noises that summer. Rather than deprive him (and the rest of the family by default) of the joy of fireworks, I purchased noise-cancelling headphones. I kept them with me for planned activities such as fireworks, so I could control the noise level for him and help him enjoy it.

Using ADHD as an excuse for not trying things would only deprive Ricochet of wonderful childhood experiences and memories. I gave ADHD grand excuse status for so long it required an enormous effort to undo it. I needed to help him find a way to thrive in anything in this world he desired to do, not just activities I deemed "ADHD-friendly."

Power to my kiddo, not his ADHD

Positive thinking truly offers a lot of power. Thinking good thoughts will make one feel better, happier, and maybe even help shape their future reality. In contrast, negative thinking can hold the same power, perhaps even greater. Negative thoughts propagate in our minds and seep and slither into every portion of our being. They can really take over our psyche if we grant them the influence.

The way I viewed ADHD, as a positive or a negative or even with indifference, greatly affected Ricochet's life, and our family. I once used the term "ADHD Monster" freely, but I stopped. Using this phrase opened the door to negativity. Debating ADHD's influence, especially in front of Ricochet, gave it legs and a life of its own. It would become part of how he saw himself and then how everyone else saw him, too. When I met with Ms. Glinda before school started his second grade year, my agenda was to say, "Ricochet has ADHD, and this is how to manage it and his behavior in your classroom." By doing so, I inadvertently set him up to be seen as ADHD first and Ricochet second. What a colossal mistake! Ms. Glinda couldn't help but approach his ADHD in every aspect of his classroom experience because I brought it to the forefront.

Self-examination lead me to realize I couldn't continue to give ADHD this sort of power over our lives. Talking about its negative attributes in front of Ricochet taught him to use ADHD as an excuse, a crutch. Instead, I needed to frequently talk about what he did well. Even further, I needed to recognize his talents and gifts and nurture them.

Sure, it's my job to help him find ways to compensate for his ADHD, to help him learn organizational skills, social skills, and how to be in control of his body, but not in the context of ADHD. It had to be approached purely as though I were teaching him everyday life skills. After all, I was teaching him life skills, just differently than I'd teach them to my neurotypical kid.

It was up to me to offer my child with ADHD an ordinary childhood to prepare him to create an extraordinary life for himself. Negativity had no place in it.

Going without an introduction

So much of life with ADHD is bittersweet. Children with ADHD are often intelligent, but struggle with school. They are creative, but don't usually get the opportunity to use their creativity in their day-to-day. They typically have kind intentions, but get railroaded by emotions outside their control. ADHD brings the bitter, but also the sweet.

Third grade was just around the corner and I was terrified, as usual! Ricochet had a well-established pattern of school struggles. Ironically, he has a gifted IQ and yet struggled to complete his classwork. Despite his kind heart and good intentions, in second grade he had been in trouble at school more often than not. School was just not good for his self-esteem, never had been. A typical mainstream public elementary classroom doesn't offer the activity and flexibility ADHD requires. My special kid's eagerness and creativity were squelched to create order and teach the facts needed to score well on end-of-grade testing.

While my mind was racing with all the things I wanted to tell Ricochet's new teacher about ADHD and his special needs, I decided to suppress it until after school started his third grade year. Talking with Ms. Glinda about his prior accommodations, classroom seating, tailored behavior plan, and more before school started turned out to be a mistake. Only a couple of weeks into the school year, I had realized she was babying him and giving him way too much rope, so to speak. He didn't have to try to complete his work and maintain acceptable behavior in her classroom, and it didn't go well.

I decided that summer that it was best not to talk to his third grade teacher about his ADHD and sensory issues until she got to know him and he got settled with her and the structure of her classroom. The year before, I inadvertently introduced my child to his teacher as a bunch of problems, before he even had a chance to introduce himself. I forced her to pre-judge him based on his differences and challenges — to see him first as ADHD.

I wasn't going to make that mistake again. Ricochet and this third grade teacher, Ms. Brash, were to get to know each other organically before I intervened.

The first week, he discovered what was expected of him in third grade and how to keep his behavior card on green, always a work in progress. She got to know the whole Ricochet: the sweet kid who had instantly decided he loved her; the active boy that fidgets in his seat; the super-intelligent kid who's great at math and science; the boy who really tries to please; the dreamer who can't always get the other boys to join him in his make-believe world; the challenging handwriting; the wandering focus; the forgetful nature; the smile that would melt anyone's heart.

It certainly wasn't perfect. After the first couple of weeks, he hadn't brought home any school communications or graded papers. He had already decided he would never get enough reward money to earn a prize he wanted because he couldn't keep his behavior card on green every day.

He did bring home one paper, titled "All About Me," in the first couple of weeks. His handwriting was on a fluctuating size scale throughout, but was legible. He even remembered to try using hyphens between his words on part of it, a strategy he was taught to increase legibility. He had about fifteen "I love..." sentences and just one "I don't like..." In it he professed his love of money, math, and his teacher. That positivity was an excellent place to start!

I sent his teacher an email asking if we could meet. I already had some concerns, such as the lack of bringing home any papers.

She responded via email, saying, "I AM SOOOOOOO GLAD YOU REACHED OUT TO ME! We should definitely meet. I have some concerns as well. How soon can you come in?"

Crap! There it was in black and white, proof that not preparing his teachers ahead of time was not the best plan of attack, either. This way, he had wasted a few weeks of school floundering because she didn't know his weaknesses and where he needed extra help. I worried that meeting new teachers before a new school year began would cause them to judge him before they get to know him, but this experience showed that's clearly better than the alternative — trial by fire and a wasted month or two. I had to find the balance between these two approaches. I needed to meet with his teachers ahead of time, but I also had to be careful to discuss his interests, gifts, and talents first, in addition to his areas of weakness. The start of a new school year was tough either way, but I decided that having a roadmap before starting that excursion was invariably prudent.

I'm a reformed helicopter momma

Hi. My name is Penny Williams... and I'm a helicopter mom.

Excuse me, I *was* a helicopter mom. I worked very hard to reform this behavior and relinquish my pilot's license. I hate flying anyway!

By definition, a helicopter parent is:

"a mother or father that hovers over a child; an overprotective parent." [7]

Yep, that was me alright. I was a master hoverer. Ricochet's ADHD counselor had been harping at me about this for quite some time.

"You need to let him fail at some point," she always said — firmly, but with compassion. "You need to step back, let Ricochet do whatever he can or will, at whatever success level comes with it, and then experience the natural consequences."

You want me to let my child fail?!

Her suggestion to *let* my child be unsuccessful certainly fell on deaf ears the first six months she tried to convince me it was a requirement. I didn't even try to refute it. To engage in conversation about it would have acknowledged such words were uttered, and I was not ready to hear that yet. I pretended she never suggested such a wicked thing.

I then debated this behavior modification proposal with her for at least another six months. I wasn't ready to accept that the best course of action for my son might actually be to sit back and watch him fail, but I couldn't resist the debate any longer.

"How does letting Ricochet fail help his already poor sense of self?" I'd argue.

"If I can help him, why wouldn't I?" I'd ask from deep within my big momma heart.

"Isn't it at the essence of a parent's job to *not* let their kids fail? Aren't I supposed to be his protector?" I'd plead.

Sitting on my hands, biting my tongue, and watching my child fail went against my very nature. I was a worrier by both genetics and environment. I've always had high anxiety, especially in social situations. My number-one motivator most of the time is fear — fear of failing, fear of being less than perfect, fear of being judged by others — we're all driven by fear to some degree, but arguably a lesser degree than I am. I cringed at the thought of my child feeling physical pain. I could be driven to tears imagining how my kids felt when their feelings were hurt. Thinking the unthinkable, kidnapping or worse, sent me straight into an anxiety-fueled tailspin. Why would I let that happen if I could prevent it? My job as momma is to protect my children, to stand firm between them and harm.

Admittedly, I had taken that philosophy too far. I was a textbook hoverer. I over-thought every scenario. I weighed the pros and cons days in advance for every situation there was even the slightest possibility might surface. I tried to anticipate the severity of the risk. For heaven's sakes, my children did not go outside to play at all the five years we lived on the mountain, because several times a year we had black bears roaming our property and traipsing up to our door. The bears never approached when we were outside. They were only around our house approximately 1/50th of the year. Those odds weren't bad, and yet I focused on the what-ifs until the thought of letting them outside seemed like child neglect or potential manslaughter by bear or something. What was I thinking? Well, I was *over*-thinking, and that's a hallmark of a helicopter parent.

Our counselor's point, though, and it was a good one, was not to push Ricochet aside and let him fail or let him get hurt. Her point was that I had to teach him the skills to work around his ADHD, and then step back and let him find his own way from there. Not only would that force him to step up and do the work, but it would also give him the breathing room to develop his own compensatory measures for ADHD. After all, kids are most successful when they do things their own way? Aren't we all?

At some point after receiving this advice numerous times over a year, I accepted the reality that I was a helicopter mom, interfering in my children's lives entirely too much. Of course, it was my job to care for them, but it was not my job to do everything for them and foresee every danger. I couldn't put them in a bubble and lock out the world so they didn't experience hurt. Hurt is a part of life, and mistakes teach us valuable lessons and make us stronger. Babying them could actually make them weak.

That revelation bears repeating: *Babying my children could actually make them weak.* That awareness was profound.

My hovering over Ricochet's every move, poised and ready to cushion his fall or prevent emotional pain, was holding him back. It also fueled arguments and power struggles. I was setting the fuse for repeat explosions.

There was a measurable improvement after I relinquished my pilot's license and stopped hovering (most of the time). Leaving Ricochet to discover and try led him to figure out how to be more like his peers in the ways he needed to be, when possible. He was happier doing things as his peers did, I guarantee. I consistently had to sit on my hands, zip my lips, and let him try.

My son was a happier kid after I quit hovering over and around him all the time. Warrior Girl was happier, too (although she quickly became aware of how much Momma really did to keep her on track). And Mr. T and I are certainly happier not feeling like we have to worry so much about the fate of our littles. While I have never had a broken bone (knocking fiercely on my wood desk right now), it is a part of childhood. *Sorry, Mom, I have to say this*, I likely didn't have this "childhood injury" because my mom was overprotective, too. Where do you think I inherited the tendency?

What doesn't kill us makes us stronger, right? Okay, let's not get carried away, I'm not ready to go that far yet! I could relinquish a lot of control without risking safety, and that's just what I did.

Is he for real?

Late September of Ricochet's third grade year, I received a call from Ms. Brash at 8:10 AM, just ten minutes into the school day and about thirty minutes after I dropped him off. She said he was hunched over a trash can, coughing. She felt like he was trying to vomit to go home from school. She was likely right. It was still a tough call, though.

His teacher asked me to speak to him.

"Your stomach will feel better in just a little while," I explained. "Let your breakfast settle."

He cried and pleaded with me, "No it won't. I feel like I'm gonna throw up. I'm not gonna feel better. Please... Please, Momma!"

I was nearly in tears, too. I was certain his stomach hurt, and I was leaving him at school, miserable, because I couldn't pick him up and teach him that a stomachache or throwing up would get him out of school. If I set that precedent, he would make himself sick every day.

I felt like the worst mom.

Just the worst.

Ricochet did vomit at school earlier that week. He was reciting the Pledge of Allegiance and threw up right in the middle of it, right where he stood. I picked him up early that day. It was just 8:15 AM. His teacher said he frequently told her his stomach hurt, but he hadn't complained that morning. He was fine after an hour at home, so I thought it was just something he ate. Later that day, he confessed that he was coughing on purpose because he missed me when he was at school. *{Sigh}*

So it was easy to see why his teacher and I thought he was working us to go home this day. Actually, I didn't doubt that he had a stomachache — we were back to Medication #3, again, and I knew it could be hard on his stomach. It also made for lousy digestion when he binged on food first thing in the morning and then the last couple hours of the day, with little or nothing in between. That was life for Ricochet on a stimulant.

This incident caused me to (again) question medication. Why was I giving him a pill that made him have continual stomachaches? Especially if he still felt so lousy at school that he was willing to force himself to vomit not to be there. What in the world was the stimulant for then? I only gave it to him for school, so he had the opportunity to achieve what his peers could achieve, have friends, and not be in trouble all the time. If he was still miserable at school, what was the point?

Each school year there was always one kid in Ricochet's class that tormented him. I felt certain he had a bully again that year, too. Different kid, same pattern of antagonizing him with constant picking.

Pick. Pick. Pick. (robbing his self-esteem)

Push. Push. Push. (until he's angry)

Take. Take. Take. (all his confidence)

He said he couldn't get away from this kid on the playground, no matter how many times he walked away. Was it possible the bully was upsetting him so much he was willing to induce vomiting to not be at school? Of course it was possible. It was probable.

My heart ached for him. It truly ached. I wanted to run into that school, scoop Ricochet up in my arms, and run out, holding him tight. Instead, I had to make a tough call — I had to leave him there to finish the school day.

Second time's a charm?

One day that October, Ms. Brash called me to discuss some concerns, and we talked for an hour. At the top of her list was emotional outbursts, which were due to a medication change. She also mentioned his writing problems. She said she spoke to the special educators and the principal to try to acquire services for him on her own, but teachers could only submit a student for evaluation every three years, and Ricochet had been submitted by Ms. Marvelous two years prior. I volunteered to make a written request for re-evaluation myself, since there's no waiting period on parent requests. That started the ball rolling for Ricochet's second evaluation.

Ricochet's problems with handwriting had been apparent as early as first grade, but he didn't yet qualify for special services and an IEP. When I thought about that rejection again, even nearly two years later, I just stared at the dust in the windowsill, gears spinning, and still with no understanding.

There I was again at the precipice of this maddening process, an evaluation for special services and an IEP. I knew the school had sixty days to evaluate, but that's all I knew. Sixty days was more than an entire grading period, a long time for a child to continue to struggle, and I just had to ride it out and take it as it came.

The process started with a meeting with two special educators, Ms. Brash, and me. I was asked to bring Ricochet's latest IQ scores in the hopes they could use those, rather than test him again at school. He tested higher the second time on the private test, showing a gifted-level intelligence, but they had denied him on the original, lower (high average) IQ scores. That history gave me mixed emotions about providing the higher score.

IQ shouldn't be a measure of academic success, and I made that argument the first time. If his IQ scores were really high, but his classroom work was much lower, didn't that automatically mean there was a problem/disconnect? He wasn't fulfilling his potential as his IQ score painted it. He was not achieving success in the classroom. Seemed like common sense to me, but tangled in the red tape of it all was that ugly beast, "good enough." The attitude that, if a student isn't failing, then he's okay. *Not!*

Unlike the time he was evaluated by the school in first grade, he was now failing in the subject of Writing. His teacher and the 504 Coordinator agreed his report card would show a "D," but his teacher made it clear that he was failing. No ifs, ands, or buts about it.

Failing.

How does a child with a gifted IQ end up failing any subject? He has a learning disability and needs help, that's how.

During the meeting, the group worked through a set of questions to determine what Ricochet exceled and struggled in to determine if an evaluation was warranted. We listed his strengths (kindness, great memory, excellent math skills, gifted intelligence) and his weaknesses (writing, planning, organizing, focus, etc.). In the end, they agreed that an evaluation was in order. That moment started their sixty-day clock to evaluate.

I found myself in this rip current once again without really knowing how to swim. My child needed a life jacket, and I didn't know how to acquire one for him. It felt like the keeper of the life jackets was determined not to give Ricochet one. That sounds dramatic, I realize, but it was exactly how I *felt*. I suspected that the IDEA (Individuals with Disabilities Education Act), the law to protect children with disabilities, was designed to support as few children as possible. Program administrators don't consider how a student qualifies for special services, but instead test and use scores to show how the student *doesn't* qualify — truly backward and asinine.

I didn't actually understand what I was asking for, oddly enough. I asked that he get services and an IEP to help him succeed in handwriting and the writing process, as both were a struggle for him. What did that get him, though? If he had a learning disability, it wouldn't be cured. He needed technology and someone to work with him in a very small group or one-on-one to complete writing tasks. If he was granted Special Education services, then what? An IEP was drafted for him. Okay. Beyond knowing that it stands for Individualized Education Program, I had no idea what it was, how it was structured, or how to be sure it was right for Ricochet. I had trouble breathing when I ruminated on that much detail.

Fortunately, Ricochet's teacher had an AlphaSmart, a small word processor often supplied to kids with handwriting disabilities, available in her classroom for Ricochet to use. If she hadn't, he would have been forced to continue to struggle many more weeks until someone granted him official Special Education status and then determined that he needed assistive technology. He was willing to use the AlphaSmart for the most part, and it had been a very positive change, helping him create legible work.

Ricochet needed more support. If it were only a problem with the physical process of writing, the accommodations under his 504 Plan would have been enough. Ricochet struggled with the writing process as well. He couldn't organize his thoughts and put them on paper. He could deliver a brilliantly imaginative story orally. Yet, when asked to write down that exact story, he would immediately state, "I can't," and become very frustrated. He really couldn't. He couldn't pinpoint where to start. Even if he recited the first sentence or two from the story again, he could not then immediately record it on paper.

I wasn't sure what they would do for this learning disability if he got services, but I hoped for one-on-one instruction and more technology. Ricochet had great ideas, and we had to figure out how to help him share them.

These were dark waters, and I was already becoming weary.

If I wrote an annual family newsletter

I thought briefly about family newsletters that December of 2010 when we received a lovely newsletter from a friend. I didn't distribute a family newsletter each year as many do. I could barely find the time and wherewithal to complete holiday cards to my business contacts, let alone personal cards and a newsletter.

I wasn't against family newsletters — it's great to keep distant relatives and friends up to date on the family happenings — it simply wasn't for me. Our family was often fueled by a comedy of errors that would read like complaints, and I would inevitably never be able to get it finished. I didn't have myself that together.

But our friend's newsletter had me thinking about how my own 2010 newsletter might have read.

Dear friends and family,

I'm sorry we haven't visited this year and have barely even picked up the phone to call. Life is so hectic and then here it is December again (and snowed in on the mountain for the fifth day in a row).

It's been a crazy year.

I don't have much time before Warrior Girl accuses me of being a mean momma or Ricochet swings from the scaffolding, which is still erect outside our home, despite moving in two years ago, so this update will be brief.

Mr. T fought lots of ice and snow January through April to get down the mountain to work and now, in December and January, he's fighting it again. He coached Warrior Girl's softball team for the third year, and learned first-hand why worker's compensation isn't as glamorous as it sounds. His hand healed remarkably after a few months, though. He's wishing Santa would bring him an iPod Touch for Christmas. Ha!

Warrior Girl grew up way too fast. She's now a tween queen, demanding her family constantly serve her, or off with our heads. She was a star softball catcher this year, as usual, and started middle school in August. Boy what an adjustment (for me)! We've had many ups and downs. She finished elementary school with straight A's and started middle school with the same. She makes us proud. Warrior Girl would like Santa to bring her a drum set, a computer (to replace the one she got for her b-day and dropped and broke), and any and all technology gadgets in existence. Good luck, Santa!

Ricochet is working on climbing his Mt. Everest (ADHD) and making slow, but steady progress. He finished off 2nd grade exceeding grade level in math and reading. He makes us proud. He played baseball over the summer, but quit after realizing he was only going to warm the bench most games. I was shamefully glad he quit — it was a terrible experience. Now in 3rd grade, he finds school much tougher. He is way less mature than his classmates and pays the price for it. He is being evaluated for Special Ed, again, for a writing-related learning disability. He uses a keyboard in the classroom to type his work already, and it helps some. He has a crush on his teacher, as he does every year, but he wishes she'd quit making him complete his work. He and Warrior Girl both had the most fun ever at a summer day camp called "Camp Invention." He's still talking about it months later. Ricochet is concerned Santa won't be able to find him in Grammie's town this year, but he would like Santa to deliver everything he's ever seen on TV to our hotel.

As usual, no time for me. Blogging big with more ADHD mommas; went to NYC for 1st time, want to go back; have more than 900 blog fans on Facebook (who'd a thunk?); had just enough real estate business to stay in the business at least a few more months; keep looking for the magic bullet to take away Ricochet's struggles; lots of therapy and doc visits with Ricochet and for myself; published a couple of articles in ADDitude Magazine; submitted an essay for a book; started having health troubles that are a mystery to my many docs and a misery to my wallet; and laughed, cried, and loved with all my heart. All I want Santa to bring me is all the gifts the three above asked for, and be sure to wrap them first, please. Oh, and we have other family here too: Grandma, Papaw, Auntie, Uncle M, and Creative H. Gotta run... so a mention will have to be good enough for them.

Wishing you more sanity than I have in the New Year,
Penny

Wow! What a year!

Developing an IEP

Just before Christmas, several weeks after the initial meeting about Ricochet's evaluation for special education services, I received an "Invitation to Conference/Prior Notice." This form officially invited the parent(s) to a conference regarding their child's special needs. It was familiar, as I'd been down this road once before, but this time there was an additional box checked off under the purpose of this meeting that had not been checked the last time — "discuss and/or develop, review, and/or revise your child's IEP." Ricochet was getting an IEP and services! My whooping echoed about the lifeless house. I was smiling so much my cheeks began to cramp. I had worked so hard for this very moment for two years.

That meeting was rescheduled four times, stretching into January, before we finally chose a day school wasn't closed due to snow. It took almost a month to make the meeting, and I held my breath the entire time. While I was ecstatic Ricochet qualified for services, I was afraid the assistive technology he required would not be offered because his elementary school had little technology. This was a new journey for Ricochet and me, having never made it past the evaluation before, so I endeavored to reserve panic for after the meeting, and only if necessary.

I attended the IEP development meeting with Ms. Brash, two Special Education teachers (who also facilitated the meeting), the school psychologist, and the school occupational therapist (OT). I could have brought others for support if I wanted; in hindsight, I wished I had asked Ricochet's therapist to attend.

The meeting started pretty rocky. I arrived at 7:30 AM as scheduled, much to my displeasure, but the team wasn't ready. The resource teachers entered at that time, but still had to set up their computer. They couldn't find the power cord for the laptop. Then they couldn't get the projector to work. All the while, one resource teacher was trying to figure out where all the other attendees were. That task was a comedy of errors in and of itself, but somehow helped me feel at ease. In their defense, we had recently lost ten days of school due to snow, including the day before, and everyone was off kilter. They finally got the computer up and running about twenty minutes after we were to start.

With the computerized form ready to complete, the psychologist and OT were still missing. By this time Ms. Brash left to try to find someone to cover her class — school was starting, and we hadn't begun the meeting yet. The resource teachers and I started drafting Ricochet's IEP alone.

It was crucial for me to understand the individual tests and what the results meant in the context of his intelligence and ability to meet his potential, as well as how these results were used to determine eligibility for services. So we first reviewed his test scores:

- hearing screening: PASSED
- vision screening: PASSED
- Woodcock-Johnson III Achievement Test: High Average is 90-109; Ricochet's scores were: Reading 116, Math 115, Reading Comprehension 110, Written Language 91, Written Expression 85
- Classroom observation by the school occupational therapist to scrutinize his hyperactivity, sensory needs, and handwriting issues as they related to classroom performance
- Intelligence Test (IQ): they used scores from private testing eleven months prior; Ricochet tested in the Gifted Range: 90-97th percentile on all areas except processing speed, which was 58th percentile. His full-scale IQ was in the 95th percentile.

Achievement Tests measure a student's academic achievement in written test format. Ricochet's scores told me that he scored high average and above in reading, math, and reading comprehension, and below average in writing. Remember that these tests were administered one-on-one in a quiet setting, with prompts to stay on task from the proctor. In my opinion, the report card was a more realistic measure of his achievement in the classroom, but it had little leverage in developing the IEP according to the law.

The Intelligence (IQ) Test is meant to measure an individual's intellectual *potential*. Again, looking at Ricochet's scores, I could clearly see that he had a gifted intelligence. Without impairment (ADHD, writing disability), he would be able to achieve A's on age-appropriate work.

There was an obvious disconnect for Ricochet between potential and performance, intelligence and achievement, even when tested in an ideal environment. His writing scores on the achievement test were below average, while everything else was above average, yet the intelligence test confirmed he had the "smarts" to achieve above average in all areas.

I didn't want the low processing speed overlooked, either. That was a very important clue as to why he had trouble finishing assignments. It also accounted for his slow reaction when spoken to — a frustrating behavior often misunderstood as defiance by teachers. Ricochet's low processing speed instantly signified that he needed modified assignments and testing environments.

I was told a good rule of thumb for judging an acceptable amount of homework was ten minutes per year of grade. For Ricochet, a third grader, he shouldn't spend more than thirty minutes on homework each day that year. That wasn't much work when accounting for a low processing speed, not to mention distractedness, lack of focus, and a learning disability.

Ricochet qualified for an IEP/Special Education based on the fact that he met the criteria for one of the fourteen disabling conditions listed in the IDEA law, the disability had an adverse effect on his educational performance, and the disability required specially designed instruction.

There was only one goal in Ricochet's entire IEP: "Ricochet will write a story with a beginning, middle, and end with 80% of the conventions correct in three out of five trials." That felt like it would require a miracle, so it certainly wasn't a goal that would be easily met to quickly dismiss him from services. I had to be sure our team was not setting goals that could be achieved in a very short period of time or didn't require enough improvement. If the goals were met, he could lose Special Education services.

I was upset he didn't have more IEP goals. Yes, writing was the biggest challenge at that time, but it was affecting his entire classroom experience, not to mention all the ADHD traits and challenges.

With this goal he was granted use of a word processor or computer access, small group pull-out with a special education teacher to work on writing skills thirty minutes daily, and OT three times in the following nine weeks. He had "General Education Program Accommodations" in every subject as well:
- multiple test sessions
- preferential seating
- student marks answers in book instead of transferring them to a bubble sheet (testing)
- testing in separate room
- modified assignments
- use of chewing gum
- use of graphic organizers

That's it? That's all two years of fighting got me? I should
have been grateful, but I wanted more. I wanted him to
have a computer for his classwork, and I wanted them to
scan his worksheets so he could complete them by typing
instead of by hand — I was already doing that for his
homework, and I knew it could be done at school, too.
There was a lot of discussion during this process, but I
didn't leave feeling accomplished. I spoke ad nauseam
about Ricochet's need to complete all work on the
computer. Ms. Brash tried to secure a computer for him
in the classroom, but was met with many excuses — it
takes an act of Congress to get a computer for the sole
use of one child. The resource teachers didn't have any
computers for their students, and told me no student
in the entire elementary school (340+ children) had
an accommodation to use a computer to complete all
assignments. *WHAT!?!*

I left the meeting feeling merely okay. We finally had
an IEP, and Ricochet was finally getting help, but my
wheels were cranking at lightning speed trying to process
it all. With every hour that passed, I came closer to the
realization that it really didn't go that well, and became
more and more upset.

I found the Assistive Technology (AT) coordinator at
our county education office a couple of days later, and
immediately fired off an email. I explained Ricochet's
special needs, all the data I compiled about certain
software that could help him, and my vision for him
to have a computer in the classroom to complete all
his work. I naively thought locating this person and
familiarizing her with Ricochet would be all that was

necessary to secure the appropriate AT. I thought she'd look at the facts, know I was right, and do the right thing for a struggling student. Uh, no; apparently it doesn't work like that. Her response was a reminder that Special Education is a system of disqualification and is designed to discover only the least they are required to provide to a special needs child. Sickening.

I'd have to wait to see if an IEP alone was really the answer for Ricochet.

Our first D

I was an A/B student growing up. I made A's and B's and did the bare minimum to get them. If straight A's were important to me, I could have worked harder and accomplished that, but B's were just fine.

A's and B's were certainly expected by my parents. Those top grades were required. Punishment always accompanied a grade of C on my report cards — my sister and I never earned a D or an F, so I can't say what the consequence for those feared letters would have been, but I assure you, the world as we knew it then would have ended. We were capable of "good" grades, and we were expected to put forth the effort to earn them.

Ricochet's second quarter report card came home a few days after the IEP meeting and blindsided me. His grades plummeted in all subjects except reading (still an A) and writing (because there's nothing lower than failing). All his behavior marks, every single one, dropped as well. I was crushed. Ricochet was crushed. And then I was pissed! Here we were with classroom accommodations, small group time in resource, and a teacher who seemed to "get it" for the most part, and the bottom still fell out. How could I be doing all the right things but everything still go so wrong?

I grew up thinking A's and B's were expected of a smart child. But now I had a super smart child, and we did not have neat and tidy A/B report cards. Ricochet got a D in the subject of Written Communication on his first third-grade report card. This D was actually an F, as his teacher had explained in our IEP meeting just prior, but apparently teachers in our area were allowed to bump it up to a D to spare a child's self-esteem. If only good self-esteem were that easy, but I'll get to that in a minute.

Anyone could tell by looking at Ricochet's report card that he was a child with learning disabilities. His report card was shouting, "Learning Disability! Learning Disability! Help me!"

I'm not referring to ADHD when I say learning disability. If ADHD were the sole problem for Ricochet, his grades would have been more consistent because ADHD is pervasive throughout all academics. It was obvious that his ADHD was somewhat well managed in this classroom because he earned A's and B's in every other subject.

My lack of control over the situation caused an overwhelming helpless feeling. Ricochet completed a year of occupational therapy for handwriting. I had already requested another evaluation for special services at school, hoping his problem was glaring enough at that point to receive services and the help necessary to discover a way to succeed in writing and earn a grade more in-line with his others.

Which brings me back to my real concern with Ricochet's D. It wasn't that he got a D. I learned long ago that grades weren't what really mattered for Ricochet. It was that he got a D when he probably did the best he could with the brain he was born with. I didn't like how upset he was about it, either.

Ricochet was with Mr. T the afternoon he brought home and saw his report card with the now infamous D on it. They looked at the report card together, and Ricochet immediately pointed out the D to his daddy. He didn't really verbalize how he felt about it, but it was written all over his face. He was obviously sad and defeated.

Warrior Girl had received her report card the day before and came home with straight A's, as she did every year before that. Ricochet received his that day too, but, in typical ADHD fashion, forgot to bring it home. I was so torn about how to praise Warrior Girl for a job well done, and yet not set Ricochet up to feel like a failure when he saw the D I knew would be tarnishing his report card. I praised Warrior Girl for a great report card, and then explained to her privately that I wouldn't go on and on about it in front of her brother, but that we were indeed crazy proud of her. (She had pulled a C at mid-term up to an A by working hard to achieve her goal.) I hate that she had to miss out on Mr. T and me jumping up and down and squealing with her, but I couldn't allow myself to indirectly make Ricochet feel worse about his grades than he already did. I refused to make him feel like a failure, even at the expense of not making Warrior Girl feel as over-the-top great as I should have. But maybe

I shouldn't have anyway because we all know straight A's aren't everything. That one little letter D broke my heart for both of them.

Ricochet resisted talking about his grades, and that was fine by me. I didn't know what to tell him or how to handle it — a D isn't okay, and yet, for Ricochet it had to be acceptable. I told him that Mr. T and I were really proud of him for doing the best he could, and that we knew his problem with writing was a difference in his brain. I assured him that we were working on trying to figure out how to help him with it. What more was there to say?

The day with the epic meltdown

This particular winter Saturday began like many. We had lots of family time planned, since we were finally getting out of the house after six long days being snowed in together, *again*. We were attending Creative H's birthday party at Chuck E. Cheese that afternoon. The kids actually looked forward to running errands after being cooped up so long, and I looked forward to a meal I didn't have to prepare nor clean up after. All family members were informed of and in complete agreement with the schedule that day.

We took it easy that morning. The birthday party wasn't until 2:30 PM, so we had the luxury of taking our time. The kids slept until they woke up naturally, and then ate breakfast at their own pace — a stark contrast to pressure-filled school mornings. They even had free time before we dressed and left the house. I drank a cup of coffee and watched the news in my pajamas, a rare treat. It was a great morning indeed.

Ricochet had been taking a lower dose of Medication #3 while home from school all week due to snow. A dose one step lower was enough to help him with impulsivity at home, but not enough of a change to throw him off kilter when he went back to his regular dose. The lower dose was certainly agreeing with him — he was full of energy and eating heartily again — and with the family. He was oozing personality, and he chose to spend more time with hands-on activities like building with Legos or modeling clay, rather than an endless parade of screen time. He was even super witty and more articulate, surprising us with some big vocabulary on a daily basis. Momma was happy, and so was he. The entire family was at peace.

We headed out around 11:30 AM, and stopped at the deli for lunch. I only had to remind Ricochet to eat a time or two, instead of the usual every thirty seconds. He was preoccupied with a table full of tiny cheerleaders, so I understood his distraction. We even ran into Ms. Marvelous whom he hadn't seen in a while. It was nice.

From there we visited my much-loved source of retail therapy, Target. The kids had two weeks of allowance burning a hole in their pockets, and each chose something to spend it on. We also picked up our usual household items. This was our second stop in a row with no arguing and no disappointment — a rare, positive retail experience. I was surprised, but knew better than to question it.

Chuck E. Cheese was loud, crowded, and overwhelming, precisely as expected. I was unsure that

Ricochet could be successful in this environment on a lower dose of medication. The pace and noise level of this venue was typically a bit agitating for him. I determined the lower dosage was great for home, but I wasn't confident it would be enough help in an over-stimulating environment like this.

Boy, was I wrong! Ricochet was a perfect gentleman — he exercised supreme patience and restraint almost throughout the entire party. He waited for all guests to arrive before playing video games, and he even stayed at the table while the other little boy (the only other boy at the party) ate his pizza, so they could play together. Toward the end of the two hours, he began to get a bit frazzled and didn't want to stop playing to watch his cousin open her birthday presents. Mr. T and I insisted because it was the polite thing to do at a party. He retorted in an angry tone and kept asking how much longer, but he recovered quickly and didn't fall over the edge into meltdown. It was a pleasant and successful afternoon.

On the way out, Ricochet exchanged the tickets he'd won playing games for trinkets. He chose only one piece of candy, knowing it all had artificial food coloring that exacerbated his ADHD in quantity. I felt there could be exceptions to the food rules from time to time, so I allowed it. I was proud of him for limiting himself to one.

We decided we wanted to eat out for dinner before returning home, but it was too early yet. I had been meaning to pop into the Goodwill stores to see if I could pick up some furniture to paint, so we decided to do that to fill the time until dinner. Ricochet ate his candy, a red

Airheads chew, on the way to the store. Warrior Girl also shared a pack of red and blue Pop Rocks with him.

The first Goodwill store was fairly orderly. We went quickly to the furniture section and left within fifteen minutes. The second Goodwill store was larger. With one foot in the door you enter a maze of shelves and shelves of trinkets, glassware, and, for lack of a better descriptor, junk. The shelves were complete chaos, and it was visually overwhelming.

Warrior Girl wanted to look for a book, so we headed for the bookshelves. I told the kids they could each choose a book or two, but that we wouldn't purchase anything else. Ricochet chose two, but Warrior Girl didn't find anything age-appropriate. I looked over the furniture very quickly and was ready to head out, but we wandered the aisles, waiting for Mr. T to emerge from the restroom. That seemingly harmless little decision turned out to be a monumental mistake.

Ricochet began to find items he felt very passionate about taking home with him. Each one was a remote-control car without the remote. I explained that they were essentially broken without the remote.

"But it's only a DOLLAR!" he'd rationalize. "I can push it on the floor. Look! The wheels still turn. It rolls!"

"No Ricochet. I explained to you when we came into the store that I would buy books, but nothing else here. You just bought toys with your allowance. What you want now is broken." I proudly remained very calm.

He bellowed a fierce groan into the air, and the books he'd chosen earlier hit the floor with force. "I don't want these books!"

There was no longer any restraint in his tone or volume. People near us were pretending to look at merchandise, but their gaze and attention couldn't help but join our escalating predicament.

Warrior Girl was fidgeting and pacing the aisles fiercely, almost as if her skin was on fire. "Daddy's back!" she exclaimed with a bit of relief.

That was our signal to leave the store.

"Ricochet, it's time to leave. I am happy to buy the books for you, or you can choose to leave without them. We need to get in line to pay if you'd like to buy the books," I explained.

"I don't want those stupid books! I want a car!"

"That's your choice," I reminded him, my voice still calm, unwavering. "Let's return the books to the shelf where you found them so we can go."

His brow was furrowed, but his eyes were wide and sinister. "NO! I'm not leaving! I'm not leaving unless you buy me that car!"

At this point, Mr. T snatched the books out of Ricochet's hands and returned them to the shelf. He came back around the corner to the tight aisle where Ricochet had planted himself between the two cars he wanted. "We're leaving now," Mr. T said sternly, and he headed straight for the exit.

I began to follow and found my load suddenly much heavier as Ricochet pulled backward on my coattail, screaming in defiance from deep within.

"I want the books! I want the books! I want the books!"

I was able to pull enough to get outside, but we were standing smack in front of the automatic doors, held open by our presence like a stage curtain for our entire Goodwill audience.

I continued to try to reason with him, explaining that his opportunity to have the books had passed, but he had already crossed the line and fallen head-first into full-blown meltdown. There wasn't any stopping this barreling train now. We had to ride it to the end of the line.

I headed for the car, and asked Ricochet to follow me. He grabbed my purse and leaned in the opposite direction with his full body. As he leaned back, our feet became entangled and we succumbed to imbalance and gravity. I'm not sure how we didn't topple to the pavement, but I managed to regain physical composure. No luck with emotional composure though — anger set it.

I had kept calm and remained rational up to this point. I knew his behavior was not within his control, that he was hyper-focused on those junk cars, and he just didn't possess the neurological skills to snap out of it and move on. But now he almost caused physical harm to both of us, a reality I wasn't going to accept. I grabbed his arm and physically escorted him to the car. Mr. T and Warrior Girl had been inside the car for several minutes now.

Ricochet and I stood behind the car as I tried to talk him down before we got in together. He was now punching me in the stomach, and repeating, "I want the books!" over and over. Tears were pouring down his face.

"I know you want the books, Buddy. I wanted you to have those books, too. But I can't buy those books for you when you were so ugly to Momma," I explained, once again. "I know you understand that."

I begged him to let me hold him and give him a big squeeze to help him calm down. We were way past that point though, and he repeatedly swatted down my outstretched arms.

Mr. T emerged from the car to use force to end the madness. I asked him to let me handle it, reminding him that I can more easily remain calm.

"He's not going to hit you and scream at you like that. I'm not having it! We need to go," Mr. T proclaimed, metaphorically putting his foot down.

Mr. T always chooses flight in a fight-or-flight situation. Always. That's just his natural reflex. Interestingly though, fleeing would end the public humiliation, but would not take him away from the problem, the rapid and disturbing melt.

He grabbed Ricochet's arms and lifted him into the car. Ricochet stretched his arms and legs out in all directions as far as he could to try to prevent it, but Mr. T got him in the car. It angered me. I didn't appreciate the physicality of his response.

I got in the front seat and sat silently.

Ricochet began to kick the back of Mr. T's seat with great power, all the while crying and repeating, "I want the books. I want the books. I want the books." On the third iteration, he would scream it from way down in his throat at the highest pitch he could reach. It was as if his brain was a record or CD stuck in a scratch, repeating the same small section of recording again, and again, and again.

Warrior Girl sat next to him in a panic. She tried to offer him everything she owned in an effort to distract him. We asked her not to interfere. We wouldn't reward his behavior, nor allow her to.

Mr. T demanded Ricochet buckle so we could go.

Ricochet silently refused.

"You can choose to be safe or not, but I'm starting the car and going home," Mr. T warned him.

Warrior Girl began to scream. "No Daddy! Buckle, Ricochet! You have to be safe. Buckle!"

She reached across him to buckle his seatbelt, but he wiggled and swatted to prevent it. She began writhing and screaming and crying. She was slipping into a panic attack and about to melt, too.

"We don't have anywhere we need to be," I reminded Mr. T. "We just need to wait it out. He's saying the exact same loop over and over, and he's obviously not in control." This was no longer a fit to get what he wanted. It hadn't been for a long while.

We sat for a minute or two longer, and Ricochet's behavior started to slowly key down. I offered him a snack, and he accepted. He was thinking of something other than the books, a clear sign he had come out of the fog. Ricochet buckled as Mr. T retrieved a snack from the trunk. Once we were all settled and ready to go, I grabbed Mr. T's hand and squeezed it. I looked up to find tears falling from his cheeks. Then mine followed.

Ricochet had melted so completely — his emotions, and all of ours, reduced to a puddle on the floor.

It took me a couple of weeks to get over the shock of that event. It was unexpected, felt tragic, and left me numb for a while. Once I gained some distance from it, I realized that the Red #40 in the candy his sister had shared with him likely led to the magnitude of the meltdown. We had discovered only a couple months prior that drinking a red Gatorade, a drink loaded with a massive quantity of the artificial coloring, caused a swift transformation that was akin to a Jekyll and Hyde moment. It truly was like that, drinking a potion and then turning beastly.

9

Fighting for a Better Reality

You must be the change you wish to see in the world.
-Mahatma Gandhi

Taking the integrative approach

Ricochet was doing a bit better with medication, therapy, and some school intervention, but not as well as I knew he could be doing. I was still in search mode and desperate for answers that would *truly* help my boy.

I had been so obsessed with ADHD since Ricochet's diagnosis that I had read dozens of books on the subject. Once I finished the doctor top-recommended books on ADHD that detail the approach to treatment of conventional Western medicine, I began to read others. (The Western approach is: If it looks like ADHD, walks like ADHD, smells like ADHD, it must be ADHD. "Get your child into therapy, and let's start trying stimulant medication to see if it will help.") At one point, his therapist put me on a self-help books restriction for a month. I read a novel for a couple of weeks, but reverted right back to reading all about ADHD — the only way I knew to find new opportunities to help Ricochet.

By reading this many books on ADHD, I started to get into the less mainstream theories and treatments. The first alternative book I read was *Healing the New Childhood Epidemics: Autism, ADHD, Asthma, and Allergies: The Groundbreaking Program for the 4-A Disorders,* by Dr. Kenneth Bock. While I found the content and his whole-body approach to treating these disorders intriguing, I felt it was a long-shot that any of his recommended testing and therapies would help Ricochet, since the cases he detailed in his book were much more profound. Our insurance wouldn't pay the thousands of dollars in medical testing prescribed in this approach, anyway.

I forced it to the back of my mind, but the longer Western medicine kept failing Ricochet, the more alternative medicine kept crying out for more of my attention. I continued to read countless similar articles on the Internet, and felt more and more that maybe there *was* more to treating Ricochet's ADHD. During this time, we continued to struggle with medication to effectively treat his ADHD. Medication #3 worked fantastically for a couple months, then swiftly lost effectiveness. He tried some non-stimulants and an antidepressant and suffered worse complications. I didn't have any idea what to do. Medications weren't working, school was getting worse, Dysgraphia was a growing complication, and our entire family was just plain unhappy and stressed out. That drove me to continue to look for alternatives.

I took note that Ricochet was experiencing some allergy symptoms, too. He had chronic dark circles under his eyes, commonly known as "allergy shiners." He also frequently had rosy cheeks and red ears, and struggled with digestive issues, too. At the same time, I read articles on food allergies and sensitivities and how they can exacerbate behavioral issues and present with these mild allergic symptoms, hard to pinpoint as food intolerance. It took a few months before I finally asked Ricochet's behavioral pediatrician about an IgG test for food sensitivities. There was a lot of debate in the medical community about whether this test was accurate, but I wanted to see the results and put the possibility of food intolerances out of my mind. IgG testing was not something his doctor was familiar with, so he referred us to the Integrative Medicine practitioner in the same office.

I knew there were many facets to the integrative approach to treating ADHD, but I had no idea how complicated and overwhelming it could be. At the first visit, we spoke about Ricochet's history and symptoms, and I gave her a copy of my medication trials chart. She exuberantly complimented my organization of all that information, while I wished there weren't so many holes in my journaling of side effects and exact trial dates.

Her first inclination was that something else was going on in Ricochet's body. There had to be a reason he tried every stimulant and some other medications for ADHD and not one had been successful for more than two months. While I was hoping to change his medication at that meeting to address a deteriorating school situation, she felt we needed to step back and look elsewhere first.

She held the medication trial chart up in front of her and toward me. "We don't want to do this to him anymore."

I couldn't have agreed more. Sharing her pointed opinion brought tears to my eyes. Of course I didn't want to keep seemingly using him as a guinea pig. *Of course! So what do we do?*

At the first appointment, the decision was made to:

- have Ricochet's blood drawn to test thyroid levels, Vitamin D, Iron, and IgG.
- keep him on the current dose of Medication #3.
- adjust his vitamins and supplements to add: a high-quality multi-vitamin, PB 8 Acidophilus, more fish oil, and a natural supplement to treat anxiety and instill calm.

We met again almost three weeks later to discuss the results of Ricochet's blood tests. Here's what she found:

- thyroid levels were normal
- vitamin D levels were low (which surprised me since he drank a ton of Vitamin D milk)
- iron reserves were low (addressed with the new multi-vitamin)
- mild sensitivity to nuts and chocolate
- moderate sensitivity to egg whites
- high sensitivity/intolerance to gluten, wheat, and oats.

There it was, my significant fear with all this testing: we needed to become a gluten-free household for Ricochet. Since the IgG test could be unreliable, I viewed the removal of gluten as a trial. If he was better without gluten, we'd know it was the right thing for him.

If not, we'd discontinue the gluten-free diet after four months. Going gluten-free was easier than I expected in some respects and much harder in others. Easier in that Ricochet was pretty agreeable to the change most of the time. We didn't have even one full-blown meltdown over wanting a food he couldn't have. He was angry the first few days, though. He even told me once, "I'll never love you again for doing this to me!" But it wasn't nearly as bad as I feared, and it improved within a week.

Cooking gluten-free was harder than I expected. I spent about $300-400 on gluten-free foods, replacing most baking items and snack foods in our pantry. I also spent $50 on two gluten-free cookbooks and felt like I needed several more. Gluten-free baking was not as simple as just swapping out traditional flour for a gluten-free flour — a mix of gluten-free flours and starches were needed for recipes to bake right, and all are not created equal. There was an enormous learning curve.

I was trying to keep change as minimal as possible for Ricochet. We had a busy evening schedule a couple of nights a week that required us to eat dinner out. We'd gone to the usual restaurants and found something Ricochet could eat (lots of cheeseburgers without the bun). We'd even had gluten-free pizza. That part was definitely easier than I expected. We were fortunate to live in a small, artsy, forward-thinking town with lots of special diet options. It would take four months of a gluten-free diet to see if it improved his ADHD symptoms though.

Next on our testing agenda was the Organic Acids Test (OAT). It measured certain enzyme levels, cell function, toxicity, etc. We were doing one test at a time, as they were expensive and insurance wouldn't touch them. This test was $240, and the IgG was about $150.

I wasn't sure if taking the integrative approach to treating ADHD would lead anywhere for Ricochet, but I felt compelled to dig deeper to see if there was more to his developmental delays. As a matter of fact, at each IEP meeting, someone said that Ricochet was a really complicated kid. Maybe there was more complexity to discover in his physiology, too.

Self-awareness is a relief

I heard a lot about self-awareness and self-regulation and how important it was for ADHD management. Quite simply, an individual can't begin to improve their behavior, unless they are aware of the behavior and how undesirable it is in the first place. Our therapist had wanted to teach Ricochet self-regulation techniques for over a year by then. I always told her he just wasn't ready. He never seemed aware of his differences and when his behavior was a problem, so we had to wait for that before teaching him self-regulation. I noticed by the end of third grade that he was recognizing when a behavior was problematic or something he just couldn't control.

One week he seemed to have an epiphany of self-awareness. Ricochet got very angry with me after school. I had a parent meeting, and he wanted to go to after care with some of his friends, but I didn't have any money on me to pay for it, and he wasn't signed up. I asked him to stay with me at the meeting. He was very frustrated, felt helpless, and began to melt down. It was a silent melt, though — a lot of sulking and pushing me away. He wasn't verbally aggressive, at least not until we got into the car and we were alone. He showed a lot of restraint, and it was great progress over where we had been.

We climbed in the car, and he started in. "You are so mean, Momma. You never let me do anything I want to do!"

"I wish I had the money for you to do all the fun things you want to experience," I answered. "But sometimes, I have to make tough decisions due to our financial situation. It really hurts my feelings when you are mad and mean toward me over something I can't afford or don't have any control over."

After about five minutes, he began to cry.

"I hate it when I'm mean to people!" he said. "I'm so sorry, Momma. I'm sorry I was mean to you. I hate it when I act like that."

I was astonished and, of course, I cried too. I felt sad for him that he couldn't control this behavior sometimes. Sad that it made him feel so sad. But I was grateful that he was aware of what had taken place. It was very clear he was finally aware of his differences and actions.

Another illustration of this self-awareness was the fact that Ricochet had been telling me, "Please don't try to change me" fairly frequently. If I asked him not to chew his fingers, stay at the table for an entire meal, or eat more at lunch, he'd say, "Stop trying to change me."

The difference in his awareness over that summer was profound. I was excited to finally start working on self-regulation with him. We started with breathing techniques to help him calm down when he was over-emotional. It would take a long time to teach him effective self-regulation, but I felt relieved that it was finally time to start. My kiddo was growing up!

The end of yet another failed school year

I worried intensely about Ricochet's school experience the last six months of third grade. Well, I've worried about it since the teacher called me on the second day of kindergarten and requested a meeting, but I was downright obsessive about it those last six months of third grade. I actually thought special services and the new IEP were the golden ticket I'd been searching for. But this is the pivotal year when students learn to work independently and become accountable, two things my special little boy was not even a little bit ready for.

Special Education didn't turn out to be a golden ticket, but rather a dripping faucet in the middle of a steamy and vast desert. The school's plan was to provide the smallest bit of help, build in baby steps, and hope that the small fraction of the day that someone was truly helping him would "spill over" into all other areas of school. No chance of that, but they wouldn't listen to me.

I fought and fought and fought. I cried in IEP meetings. I sent stern emails to the Special Education staff at the Board of Education. I trolled the Internet for advice from advocates. Ricochet's mainstream public school was a fine school with very nice teachers and administrators, but they weren't able to give him an active learning environment. He needed a school that understood invisible disorders like ADHD, SPD, executive functioning deficits, and different learning styles, and he needed to be reminded how smart and wonderful he is, not (inadvertently) reminded that he was very different.

I put Ricochet into the enrollment lotteries for two local charter schools, and I applied at two private schools, one specifically for language-based learning disabilities, and one that was just small and focused on experiential learning. The private schools would require hefty financial aid, but I figured I wouldn't know if that was possible unless I asked.

Ricochet's enrollment number didn't get selected for either of the charter schools (there were only a few openings in each entire school). We were turned down for the learning disabilities school because the director felt he would be bored there in remedial math and reading when he only had a learning disability in writing. But Ricochet was accepted to that small private school with an emphasis on experiential learning and science; I'll call it School Oh-No from here on.

I had enrolled Ricochet in School Oh-No for the following academic year. This school was better geared to his learning style with a student-to-teacher ratio less than half of that in his current school. I knew it was going to be better for him. And yet, I wasn't worrying any less. While I was not as worried about school for Ricochet at that point, at least not until the new school gave me a reason to worry, there was an endless supply of things for a worry-wart like me to be consumed by. I guess it was the overwhelming desire to fix something that can't ever truly be "fixed."

Accepting that ADHD really is a disability

When Ricochet was diagnosed with ADHD, I denied the term "disability." The first three years after Ricochet's diagnosis, I claimed over and over again that I viewed ADHD as a difference, not a disability. I truly believed that and never used the word "disability" to describe my son. He's intelligent and creative, fun and capable — not at all disabled. I guess I didn't fully understand the term.

Merriam-Webster defines disability as: "a disqualification, restriction, or disadvantage." I wish someone would have reminded me of that broad scope when Ricochet was diagnosed — maybe I wouldn't have walked around with blinders on for several years.

One day, I realized that ADHD (and Sensory Processing Disorder/SPD and learning disabilities) was really a *disability* that causes my son to be different, not simply a difference. Did I then walk around talking about how he's disabled? No, of course not. But I finally saw it clearly. I hoped this clarity would permit me to truly accept him the way he was and no longer work so hard to figure out how to "fix" his ADHD, which was really only trying to change him.

I came to this realization with a good, old-fashioned kick in the pants, of course. Toward the end of that summer, Ricochet had been gluten-free for about four months. I decided it was time to test how much the diet change was doing for him by taking a medication break. It was incredibly eye-opening, but not at all in the way I expected.

While I'd known for some time Ricochet's medication wasn't doing enough, I truly didn't realize how much benefit he still got from taking it. Even he would tell me each day without medication that he liked not swallowing the pills, but felt more in control and calmer when he took his medication. Even this immature then eight-year-old could tell the medication was affording some positive improvements for him.

Ricochet didn't take his medication for a full week that summer. Most days we didn't have anywhere we had to go, thank goodness. But on day six, we decided to embark on a mini family road trip. We hiked up to Mt. Mitchell's lookout tower, and then followed the Blue Ridge Parkway on around to Little Switzerland for dinner. This was a trip we'd made before and a trip Ricochet enjoyed. But this time, the entire forty-five minute drive there, he asked when we were going home. He didn't want to go anywhere at all. He didn't have the patience for the car ride, even with electronics to keep him occupied.

The true epiphany was at dinner. Little Switzerland is this teeny-tiny town in western North Carolina on the Blue Ridge Parkway. If you blink, you will miss it, I swear. There's a small, old general store and restaurant there that we like. It's casual, filled with history and character, and they make a wicked-good smoked trout BLT sandwich.

Ricochet was super fidgety in the restaurant, falling out of his chair over and over again, and his voice was loud, too, but I thought he was doing well otherwise. Then a boy a year or two *younger* sat down with a group of ladies at the table next to us. This boy sat still and quiet and drew on a piece of paper the entire time. The stark contrast between Ricochet and this other boy nearly blew Mr. T and me right out of our chairs. I'm afraid we probably stared at that boy. We were dumbfounded, but knew that the other boy was behaving as expected for his age — our child was the one who was not typical.

Our hearts broke that evening. We recognized that Ricochet truly is disabled, even if only in some respects. He didn't have the ability to sit still in the chair, regulate his voice, or simply act his age, especially not without medication. It was clear that his medication was helping some and that the gluten-free diet was not the answer to treat his ADHD.

My second reminder that Ricochet is disabled came only a few weeks later when Ricochet's teacher at School Oh-No told me he was inattentive, not completing his work, and disrupting the group sometimes. I was stunned. I didn't think we were going to have the same issues in this hands-on learning environment. But of course we would, because these are deficits in Ricochet's abilities that don't magically go away simply because we alter his environment.

My son has a disability (many, in fact). I'm glad I finally made peace with it so I could stop working so hard to change those deficits and focus on teaching him how to be happy and successful despite them.

What the hell was I thinking?

I had lived in search mode ever since Ricochet was diagnosed with ADHD in 2008. I searched for the medication, therapy, classroom accommodation, and/ or product that would make his life with learning disabilities a little easier. I guess you could say I was searching for the magic bullet, but I don't think that's accurate anymore. It was true the first year or two — I was looking for an "answer," a "fix," something to erase his ADHD symptoms. Then I realized that "something" doesn't exist. I didn't think I was looking for a cure for ADHD, because I knew that was impossible, but that's exactly what I was searching for nonetheless.

My search focus became more refined. I started looking for tools to help him compensate for his differences, for environments where he could learn and prosper, for parenting methods best suited to his needs, and treatments that taught him the skills necessary to have a happy, successful life despite ADHD (and Dysgraphia, Written Expression Disorder, SPD, executive functioning deficits). This search was intense and stressful. There's a lot of (self-inflicted) pressure to be diligent to find all opportunities and to make choices that will only have positive outcomes. In the area of making appropriate choices that lead to positive outcomes, I failed miserably in 2011.

Ricochet had struggled in school since the day he walked into kindergarten. While it should improve each year with treatment, maturity, growing self-awareness, and a diligent advocacy for accommodations and resources in school, it had not improved much for Ricochet. By the second semester of third grade, I felt like we had been standing in the same place for three years, paralyzed, while the world continued to move on all around us. We were moving and working, but getting nowhere.

I fought hard with Ricochet's school for an appropriate educational environment for him, but mostly received lip service. I watched Ricochet struggle to fit in an environment that was clearly the opposite of what he needed. I knew he needed more help if he was to have any chance at academic success. I had tasked myself with finding that for him, and felt certain School Oh-No was the answer.

Ricochet was ecstatic to attend School Oh-No. Mr. T and I were ecstatic, too. The school looked so fantastic from the periphery that even Warrior Girl was jealous. We couldn't afford the tuition in full and didn't receive scholarship, but we received a small settlement from a work injury Mr. T suffered the year before, just enough to bridge the gap between the annual tuition and what we had available to spend on it. It was exactly what I wished for. It seemed like a sign from the universe that Ricochet was meant to attend this school. Ricochet's new teacher and I discussed his needs at length the day he came to hang out in her classroom before being accepted and enrolled. Plus, I submitted all evaluation reports, as well as his former 504 Plan and IEP with the private school application. Everyone understood his needs and expressed nothing but confidence that Ricochet was going to thrive and flourish at School Oh-No.

Things began falling apart the first week. Ricochet kept telling me everything was great, and he was happier than I'd ever seen him, but his teacher painted a darker picture.

"He needs a personal assistant," she whispered toward me in the hall one afternoon as if it were some shameful secret. "He requires someone guiding him through things at every moment. I don't feel qualified to teach him."

The first week of class at School Oh-No, I was told the teacher didn't feel qualified to teach my son. Apparently, I thought I could teach her to teach him, because I didn't pull him out and run right then.

If I hadn't been so blinded by hope, I might have seen that day that it wouldn't work out with School Oh-No. But I was blinded. I put a plan in motion to determine appropriate accommodations in the new school environment and shared them with the school. I met with his two teachers once, and then it escalated to a meeting with the Headmaster and the Admissions Director. The Headmaster was very positive in that meeting, acknowledging Ricochet's different needs with very educated and clear understanding. He gave the teachers suggestions on how to mitigate his challenges and their potential disruption to their classroom.

My hope shone even brighter that this school was indeed the best place for Ricochet.

Then, just a week later, I was asked to meet the group again the next day, a full seven days earlier than the originally agreed meeting schedule. I felt sick to my stomach. My head throbbed incessantly. I knew all too well what was coming, and I couldn't stop it.

I sat down at the meeting table in the Headmaster's office that morning and took out my notes from our last meeting. They all watched me intently. I settled, then noticed no one else had even a pad of paper. The tension and stares drove me into a slump in my chair. I laid my pen gently on the table — I obviously wasn't going to need it.

The Admissions Director started the meeting. "We can't teach Ricochet here."

I felt my emotions welling out of control, so I interrupted her. "I am going to get very emotional, and I can't help it." I barely made it through that one sentence audibly before the blubbering started.

"I recognize that you gave us adequate information on Ricochet's needs during the admissions process. You should find him a private teacher. Can't you do that? That's what he really needs," she continued unsympathetically.

Who could afford that? I screamed in my head. Certainly not my family.

The Headmaster stepped away to look in another room for some tissues, but brought back just a small, thin piece of toilet paper. The irony of me holding that small strand of toilet paper to my wet face, inconsolable, as they went on about how Ricochet didn't fit in their school was apparent to me even amidst the emotional chaos. The meeting was belittling, and the sopping toilet paper held to my face was a clear illustration of that.

They continued on very coldly, showing no emotion. They were all three heartless or had rehearsed this meeting together prior. Maybe both.

"We can write some sort of letter for his school if it would be of any benefit," she added.

What the hell will that accomplish?!

I couldn't speak. I could barely keep from blubbering like a child. A piece of me broke into bits and was stranded at that table that day, while my sweet son sat in a classroom above us, deliriously happy and completely oblivious that he was being rejected. I was told my child was "too disabled" for something, and that cut deep.

Just two months into his fourth grade year, they asked me to remove Ricochet from School Oh-No. They said he could stay for two weeks longer, but Ricochet never returned to School Oh-No after Mr. T picked him up that afternoon. Ricochet was devastated. He loved School Oh-No with all his heart. Despite not being able to accommodate his special needs, it was the perfect school environment for him, and he knew it. I was deliberate in explaining that leaving School Oh-No was not a choice that Mr. T and I made. I didn't want him to blame us for his pain. I also made it clear to him that he did absolutely nothing wrong, and he didn't — he was just himself.

I asked School Oh-No to refund our entire tuition on the grounds that we entered the enrollment process and contract with full disclosure and they did not (their parent handbook, not provided to us until after school had started, stated that they don't teach special needs children). They sent a check that covered most of it, despite an enrollment contract with our signatures that said they didn't have to.

Ricochet stayed home with me for a week to recharge and give the unexpected changes time to settle. He then went back to the public elementary school he had attended the three years prior. The school welcomed him with open arms, and he was excited to see old friends.

Ricochet was happy there for a while. Almost as happy as at School Oh-No, it seemed. We later discovered in a session with his counselor that he had been concealing extreme feelings of inadequacy at School Oh-No because he loved the exploration and intense science emphasis. I guess it all settled where it was meant to in the end.

Guilt consumed me, though. I worked like a pit bull to find an alternative educational experience for him. I fought when we didn't have the money for it. I made it work, even though I knew it would mean some tough financial sacrifices for the entire family. I put Ricochet in a situation that ultimately led to very intense heartbreak. I hurt him instead of helping him, and had a really hard time forgiving myself. Good intentions just weren't enough sometimes.

My theory of relativity

"It's all relative." The scattered genius, Albert Einstein (who is believed to have had ADHD and learning disabilities), said so himself. He was referring to reference points in space, but it applies to everything in life, really. Our opinion or definition of any one thing depends on our frame of reference and our vantage point. To illustrate very simply: I personally think $10,000 is a heck of a lot of money. Someone who is wealthy might think it's very little. I have real estate clients who are easily willing to risk that much and more. One man's pocket change may be another's pot of gold — because it's all relative to one's perspective.

I realized that relativity had played an ever greater role in my psyche since Ricochet was diagnosed with ADHD. I often found my inner voice reminding me that things could be worse. The realization that Ricochet's life (and my own life) could be harder revealed a lot of opportunities for gratitude, often in the littlest of packages.

That year in particular had been a really tough year for Ricochet and a really tough year to be his (adoring) momma. We discovered that he must adhere to a gluten-free diet, as it helped him in ways other than behavior. He continued with failed medication trials, nearing the end of possibilities for effective medication to treat his ADHD. I battled with Ricochet's public school for assistive technology and more classroom accommodations and lost. We put him in a private school, despite not having the tuition in our budget, and he was asked to leave within two months. Our family was entering financial hardship with no end in sight. There was a lot to worry about, but I made a conscious effort to focus on the positive — for Ricochet and for our family.

There truly was much to be thankful for. I had a sweet and loving kid who was bright and full of kindness. He had an amazing heart and wonderful creativity. I found myself noticing all of his great qualities more and more the harder everything else got, thanks to relativity. I was thankful for that, too.

Momma bear attacks when provoked

School. *Argh!* Truly the bane of my existence. I spent more energy trying to achieve school success for Ricochet than on anything else, even more than on my business at times. The emotional distress I endured while begging school staff to understand and accept my son's challenges, to work with his differences instead of against them, was mind-numbing.

School problems started to bubble to the surface again after Ricochet had been back at public school for a few months since leaving School Oh-No. Ricochet's new teacher, Miss Gulch, firmly believed that if he produced less written work than his peers, he would actually learn less. She believed that he must continue to take tests and quizzes in multiple-choice, hand-written format, or he wouldn't be able to pass end-of-grade (EOG) tests and move on to fifth grade. Students don't have to pass EOGs to be promoted to the next grade, actually, and I had the principal tell her so in a later meeting.

A few weeks after Ricochet returned to the public school, we had an IEP meeting to refocus. Two weeks later, after receiving a mid-term report that generically stated that Ricochet needed improvement in all academics and in all behavior areas, I probed Miss Gulch to find out what Ricochet's grades looked like. It took two or three emails asking directly if Ricochet was going to receive any F's on his report card to get her to finally answer the question. And the answer was yes, in Reading.

Reading? What?! How is that even possible? This kid has an IQ in the 130s, he was reading at a sixth-grade level in fourth grade, according to their benchmark testing, and his learning disability was Dysgraphia, a disability of handwriting and written expression, *not* reading. If this smart, kind kid had an F in Reading, the school was failing him. Yes, I'm quite serious, it was most definitely the school's fault.

The main reason for the F on his upcoming report card was that he had failed every single reading comprehension test. I asked Ricochet to give me more information about these tests, and quickly realized he didn't have the level of executive functioning skills required to complete this type of test format with success. These tests were four pages of multiple choice questions and three short-answer questions after a short story, printed front and back and stapled. Writing out answers in sentence format wasn't the problem either, as I first suspected. The problem was that he had to go back to the text to find the answers to the multiple-choice questions. Ricochet couldn't read a question on a print-out, move back to the first page and look for the answer, remember what he was looking for while searching, then remember the answer and find his place in the test again to mark the answer. This was far too much for his brain to handle from an organizational standpoint, but especially with poor working memory. Yes, his memory was off the charts when he was tested, but the part of his memory employed when carrying out tasks suffered tremendously, part of his executive functioning deficits.

With that information, I quickly notified his Special Education teacher, and asked for another IEP meeting as quickly as possible. IEP meetings terrified me — historically, they had never gone my way. In first grade, he was tested and denied Special Education inclusion, no matter how many people I reasoned with. In third grade, he was retested and granted Special Education inclusion for writing, but he only had one goal, based entirely on writing mechanics. And, no matter how many IEP meetings I called and how hard I fought to convince the group of his deeper struggles with executive functioning deficits, the IEP never changed. We discussed ideas and accommodations with majority agreement, and then time and time again nothing was implemented. None of these ideas were ever added to his IEP document, so I couldn't fight for justice when agreed-upon accommodations never came to fruition.

In an IEP meeting the prior year in third grade, Ms. Brash looked me in the eye across the table, and said, "You have to accept that your child's life is going to be hard. He was born that way, and you can't fix it. We can't all bend over backward to try to make it less hard."

When I returned to the table from balling my eyes out in the hallway after her pointed comment, I was patronizingly told, "It's obvious you love Ricochet very much."

This was their way of saying that my expectations were too high because I was biased as his momma — that I was looking for perfection because I was blinded by love. Every accommodation I asked for had turned up in my research, they were wrong about that, but it didn't matter because I was just his momma.

I was determined to be heard this time, so I brought backup — Ricochet's therapist. I was going to have these recommendations come from outside professionals, rather than just his momma this time.

Ricochet's therapist attended the first half of the meeting. She tried to reason with Miss Gulch about the fact that, no matter how hard he tried or how much he was pushed, Ricochet would never be able to match his peers in all aspects because he has a "brain disorder that can't be changed." I also had a report from a Special Education teacher turned Educational Advocate who looked over Ricochet's existing IEP, his current schoolwork and grades, and spoke to me about his strengths and weaknesses, to develop recommendations for Ricochet to be able to achieve academic success. Her report was distributed to the full IEP Team (Miss Gulch, two Special Education teachers, the gifted teacher, the principal, the school OT, the school social worker, our private counselor, and me) in advance of the meeting.

This strategy seemed to work. While none of us could convince Miss Gulch that Ricochet needed modified assignments and testing, it was added to his IEP nonetheless, forcing her compliance. Yes, forced — I had to speak with the principal about it just a couple days after the new IEP was drafted. In addition to Ricochet's goal for writing mechanics, a goal for organizational skills and a plan to help him develop these skills was added. As well, he had many new accommodations, such as: full testing accommodations, allowing him to test away from the classroom; modified assignments; and extended time.

The battle didn't end there with the rigid Miss Gulch. By pushing him to be just like his peers, despite the fact that he physically couldn't, Miss Gulch created an environment where it was impossible for him to achieve and where he always felt inferior. She pushed Ricochet so hard to be just like his peers that his anxiety welled to an explosive point. One Friday, while Miss Gulch was absent, ironically, the class had an auction to purchase toys with their behavior tickets. Mind you, Ricochet could not earn even half as many tickets as his classmates, and then he couldn't keep track of what he did earn up to auction day. He had four tickets that day when the majority of the students had twenty or more. When a friend bid higher than he could on a toy he wanted, Ricochet had a full-blown meltdown — his first ever at school.

His explosion was so great — pushing over desks and chairs — that the classroom had to be emptied for the safety of the other students until the principal could calm Ricochet down and get him to leave the classroom.

I was eventually called and told what happened. The principal offered for Ricochet to go home early if I wanted him to. She never said one word to me about his behavior being unacceptable or about punishment for his actions. She simply told me the facts of what had transpired, her compassion transferring right through the phone.

Mr. T raced right up to the school to pick up Ricochet because I had a meeting with a client. He found a weary, sad shell-of-a-boy sitting alone in the school office. His eyes were red from crying, and he barely uttered a word for several hours. He was completely devastated and humiliated. This outburst was the furthest thing from his sweet personality, and we all knew he had no control over it, even the school principal.

I told everyone that school escalated Ricochet's anxiety ten-fold that year. We even went to a psychiatrist through the school who confirmed it. Then Miss Gulch would say that Ricochet was fine in her class, that he didn't complain about anything and was just telling stories at home. He didn't tell her anything because *he was deathly afraid to*. This incident proved his anxiety was at a boiling point.

The following Monday, before I could even initiate a meeting about the incident, Miss Gulch made Ricochet stand up in front of the entire class and apologize for "having a temper tantrum" that Friday. The minute I heard about that I was on the phone with the principal. This incident was most definitely not a "temper tantrum." This was a meltdown, common of kids on the autism spectrum. This was a million miles from a "tantrum." Miss Gulch had crossed the line into legal discrimination, and I was fully prepared to file a complaint of discrimination with the US Office of Civil Rights. I sent a scathing email to everyone at the school who had contact with my child explaining the difference between a "meltdown" and a "temper tantrum" and unmistakably demanded an apology. Not an apology to Mr. T or me. Miss Gulch was going to apologize to Ricochet! And I wanted the apology to take place in front of the whole class, so his peers would understand what had truly happened and not think he was a fourth grade baby who has "temper tantrums."

The apology never came. Miss Gulch became very adversarial toward me, not that I was surprised. The Special Education staff and the administration continually told her she must comply with the accommodations in the IEP, and she continually refused shamelessly.

My threatening email incited the principal to order a Functional Behavior Assessment, though, and she put a rush on it. The following week, we all met again, but this time a Behavioral Specialist facilitated the meeting, my Wonder Woman. We gathered in the library, waiting for the prior meeting to end so we could get started. I kept looking at my watch, and Wonder Woman said, "Don't worry, this will only take an hour." I may have rolled my eyes, but I tried not to. She had obviously never been in a meeting about a special needs student opposing Miss Gulch.

I wish I could place my subsequent conversation with Miss Gulch word-for-word on this page, but time and the intense emotions of that day have blurred the details. I brought the current project assignment sheet with me to discuss with Miss Gulch. The students were to mail five hand-written letters requesting information to five Chamber of Commerce offices in North Carolina, each with a Flat Stanley they handmade tucked inside. The grades were based on the number of letters they sent and the number of responses they received to their letters — the second, a criteria that was 100% out of their control.

I questioned Miss Gulch about it, explaining that it was very hard for Ricochet to write these letters due to his Dysgraphia, and that we had no way of controlling responses. I let her know I felt it was unfair for any of her students to get a C on this project only because none of their recipients responded. I explained to her that Warrior Girl did the same project with a different teacher three years before, and they only mailed one letter and completing that one ensured a good grade. She said she expected more of her students because she knew they were capable of more, citing that her classroom was full of gifted students. I asked her to modify the assignment for Ricochet, as it stated in his IEP, and allow him to write fewer letters, but still fulfill expectations to earn a good grade. She refuted my appeal, offering her opinion that my request was unfairly changing the grading scale only for Ricochet.

I don't remember my exact response. I was overcome with rage and spoke firm and decisively. I let her know that having a gifted intelligence doesn't mean that you can or should do a larger volume of work. And I reminded her that she was obligated by law to follow the guidelines laid out in Ricochet's IEP, including the accommodation for modified assignments. I was so forceful and educated in my response that Wonder Woman, whom I had never met before, stopped what she was doing in her day planner and looked up at me. Her face shone with approval — not at all the reaction I expected for raising my voice to a teacher.

Fortunately, we were called into the meeting room before my discussion with Miss Gulch could get any more heated. As we filed into the room, I turned to Wonder Woman, and whispered, "You have no idea how happy I am that you are here."

She responded with a simple wink.

The meeting that Wonder Woman was sure would only take an hour lasted nearly four. As with all other IEP meetings with Miss Gulch, she refuted each suggested strategy and accommodation at great length, and then refused implementation. At one point, Wonder Woman pounded her fist to the table and told her point-blank and with a severe tone that she didn't have to agree with anything being said in that room that day, but she still had to follow his IEP to the nth detail because it was the law.

Moments after that, as Miss Gulch refuted yet another behavioral strategy, I fell over the edge. I stood up, turned toward her, and began yelling at her. Truly yelling. I don't remember at all what I said, but it's the only time in my life I can remember yelling in the face of someone who isn't part of my inner circle. I am a pacifist, and I had never before been pushed that far with an acquaintance. The principal remained quietly seated and let it play out. She knew I was right. She knew the teacher deserved it. She knew she could not defend her on this point. Wonder Woman quickly wrapped up the meeting.

Life in Miss Gulch's classroom remained unchanged. When I incessantly pushed her on reducing his assignments, she pushed back until we came to blows. I told her that her workload was insane for any fourth grade child. I reminded her she was to reduce the magnitude of assignments for Ricochet per his IEP, which was enforceable by Federal law.

She then fired back, in writing to be memorialized for all time, "I'll just put an A in my book for this project since that's what you want."

I responded to her email, copying the principal and stating that I had never insinuated nor asked her to fudge Ricochet's grades, and I hadn't. I reiterated that my goal, as well as the goal of the Special Education department, the principal, and his IEP document, was to level the playing field for a child with disabilities. That email went back and forth about five or six times, more heated with each rebuttal. She even went so far as to tell me that she obviously thought more highly of Ricochet's abilities *than his own mother!* Flames shot out my ears, daggers from my eyes. That was way over the line. I waited silently for the principal to step in.

Two days later, on a Friday afternoon, the principal called. She suggested we move Ricochet to another classroom on Tuesday, at the start of the last grading period. I hesitated. What the hell was wrong with me?

The worst year ever!

I'd been through hell's entry fire and back a hundred times with Miss Gulch over the middle six months of Ricochet's fourth grade year, but I hesitated about moving Ricochet to a new classroom so late in the school year, after he'd already been through an entire school change, too. I worried about his self-esteem and how the (mean) kids would react. I worried that Ricochet wouldn't want to move — after all, he thought Miss Gulch was wonderful because he gives everyone the benefit of the doubt. I saw the anxiety caused by this stubborn teacher taking over his thoughts, emotions, and even his physicality, but I hesitated to move him to a new classroom so late in the school year. I wanted to do the right thing for Ricochet, not the right thing for me or anyone at the school. The principal assured me they would handle any fallout of the move and protect him. *Bless her heart!* She confided that she had never moved a student that late in the school year in all the years she'd been in administration. She also retired after that year. Who could blame her?

Ricochet moved across the hall that following Tuesday.

What a difference the (right) teacher makes! I can't begin to describe the relief that Ricochet experienced. Our whole family felt some relief, especially me — I got my life back.

Ms. Splendid, Ricochet's new teacher for the remainder of the year, got it. She truly got it. She understood him. She understood his behaviors were signs, triggered by his lagging skills or his different needs. She appreciated that there is more than one way to learn and more than one way to show what you've learned. She understood we don't all fit in a neat little box.

She. Got. It.

This teacher had wings.

To illustrate the stark contrast between these two teachers, I'll describe our latest IEP meeting with the new teacher. The IEP team had a Functional Behavioral Assessment (FBA) follow-up meeting with the new classroom teacher, Ms. Splendid. {swoon}. The meeting took less than an hour. She agreed with everything everyone said. She hadn't seen the FBA strategy chart we made in the first meeting, and yet, when we reviewed the strategies to see if they were beneficial, she was already implementing just about every one of them from her own intuition. I loved this woman!

The real test of the efficacy of this change was Ricochet. He was doing marvelously. I could see relief wash over him after the first day in the new classroom — his body was more relaxed, his mood was lighter, and he actually said he had a good day. After seeing him in the new classroom, everyone saw he had been really suffering with Miss Gulch.

Was life in the new teacher's classroom perfection? No. But that's not about her. Ricochet has ADHD and learning disabilities; it has never been about perfection.

We requested that Ricochet repeat fourth grade after that tumultuous year, with his eager approval. He was actually ahead of grade level, but we pushed for retention because he had the toughest year ever, and he was immature and far behind socially. He needed to be with students who were more like peers. He needed a chance to catch his breath.

10
A fresh start

"A bridge of silver wings stretches from the dead ashes of an unforgiving nightmare to the jeweled vision of a life started anew."
— Aberjhani, The River of Winged Dreams

Recovering forward momentum

I learned an interesting sailing term recently — "in irons." When you are in irons, you are sailing against the wind so directly that the boat stalls and is unable to maneuver. You are stuck, to put it quite simply. It requires calculated maneuvering to recover movement.

ADHD and learning disabilities put Ricochet's boat in irons more times than not for several years, and I was often on the boat with him. The first three years after diagnosis, I read just about every book on ADHD and stayed the course just as it was mapped. I did everything I knew to do, and still didn't experience much forward momentum when it came to the treatment and management of Ricochet's ADHD.

We were often in irons.

I was exhausted and weary.

I made a concerted and calculated effort to push forward nonetheless and fight for a better reality. I was forever determined to turn this thing around and help Ricochet catch his tailwind.

After a few years collaborating with Ricochet's behavioral pediatrician to test just about every medication, dosage, and combination possible, we finally stumbled upon treatment success. We repeatedly went back to Medication #3 because he tolerated it well and it worked great when it worked. The idea was to keep trying additional medications with it, which we did until we happened upon a blend that sustained efficacy for Ricochet's ADHD symptoms. It was the spring of 2012, three and a half years after diagnosis.

After trying all medications approved for ADHD and most medications commonly prescribed when the standards weren't appropriate, Ricochet's doctor began reaching for solutions. Having been in the industry for decades, he knew of a little-known drug originally approved in the 1960s as a treatment for influenza of all things, but later discovered effective in reducing the symptoms of Parkinson's, a neurological disease affecting movement. Ironically, it's no longer prescribed for influenza because all current strains of the virus are resistant to it. It isn't known exactly how it works on the symptoms of Parkinson's, but it is believed to boost the effects of dopamine, a neurotransmitter often off-kilter in the brains of those with ADHD, too. This medication was sometimes prescribed to individuals with ADHD with success so I agreed to try it with Ricochet.

We quickly found that this medication didn't provide enough ADHD symptom control on its own, but it augmented his stimulant medication beautifully. I held my breath the first few months, waiting for it to lose efficacy again, but it never happened. Almost two years later, he still takes this medication twice a day with a long-acting stimulant, and it is still the best treatment Ricochet has had. He is more attentive and calmer and less impulsive, while still able to be his happy-go-lucky, sweet, and charming self, most of the time.

We were finally learning how to turn ADHD lemons into something more akin to lemonade. The recipe is not an inventory of concrete measurements, but rather a malleable list calling for a little of this and more of that. Sometimes, this special lemonade turns out better than others.

Ricochet's treatment team and I finally had his boat out of irons and traveling a forward trajectory. That felt incredible, yet I knew I couldn't let my guard down. Treating ADHD was often like aiming at a moving target.

Our lost summer

The summer between Ricochet's fourth grade years was tumultuous for our family. Not due to ADHD, learning disabilities, or differences between my kiddo and the "norm," but life and a whole big load of uncertainty taking over.

We got our home on the mountain under contract to sell that June. The frantic search for a new home to purchase ensued immediately. It took over every moment of free time Mr. T and I had. Not only did we look at house after house, trying to find the perfect blend of budget and livability for our family, but we spent a lot of time in the car — we were moving all the way across town, about forty minutes from our soon-to-be old house.

I do not exaggerate when I say the search consumed us. I worked from home while Mr. T was at work. The kids watched TV, played games, and not much else (remember, this is the home with bears and they couldn't just go outside and play). There were a few occasions when I could take them to the pool or to visit friends, but a scarce few.

There went the month of June... and part of July. Exhaustion penetrated every pore — more from stress and anticipation of the unknown than from physical tiredness. But exhaustion, nonetheless.

We spent July packing. We moved in with my parents for what was supposed to be two weeks on July 12, the two weeks between closing the sale of our old home and purchasing the new one. Over a month later we were still living with my parents.

{Sigh}

Lost. Summer.

We visited our dogs at the kennel at least once a week for the sake of the kids, as well as the dogs. The sale of our home became drastically delayed, but we had already moved out. Moved across town. Moved to a new (better for Ricochet) school district. We didn't feel that there was any turning back. The move was a decision to better our family life and, by golly, we were going to make it work no matter what. My parents so graciously let us invade their clean, personal, quiet space for an indefinite amount of time.

Our children were not sleeping in their own beds. 99% of their stuff was in a storage shed down the street. Their dogs were in a kennel down the street. They were dreading starting over at new schools where they didn't know anyone. They no longer had cable/satellite TV. Life as they knew it had changed. Drastically! And we were not certain of the future.

The buyer of our home was trying to work things out with his lender, but it was going to take a month or more. The seller of the home we were under contract to buy was uncertain that our home would sell so we could buy his home. Now he was waiting for it to close before he moved out.

We couldn't define expectations. We didn't know what to expect. We continued to putter around in a house that was not our home, without our creature comforts, seemingly stuck in the muck the rest of the summer. Totally lost.

Mr. T and I were determined the kids were going to attend school in this new district, and so we sent them to new schools, despite not knowing our residency fate. We decided that change was non-negotiable.

Our sale and purchase both closed six weeks after we moved in with my parents. We still had to stay with them another two weeks before we'd move into our new home.

We (finally) moved in and worked on crafting our new normal and settling our new nest.

This lost summer held way too much unknown for a child with ADHD. Ricochet needed clearly-defined expectations and to know what was coming next and when. This sort of paralyzing muck could have been catastrophic.

And yet, it wasn't.

Ricochet did remarkably well. He never once asked me to go get a specific toy out of the storage shed (thank goodness, it would not have been possible). He never once cried for his own room or his own bed. He didn't seem to mourn the loss of what he knew. I can't say it transpired without incident, though. He was more emotional than usual. I know I was, too. He had a full-blown meltdown in the Dairy Queen one Sunday when Grandma and Papaw took their grandkids for a treat. He had a small emotional meltdown when I walked him into school on the second day, nervous about the unknown, afraid he'd be in trouble a lot there just like his old school.

But we worked through all those things. We were so lucky that Grandma and Papaw worked to truly understand Ricochet and accept him for who he is. I worked with his teacher to help him settle at the new school.

The new house would be fantastic for Ricochet... and the whole family. We moved into a real neighborhood, with mostly-level paved streets to walk and ride bikes on. There's a small playground and many kids in the neighborhood. We had a fenced yard that created the perfect scenario to send Ricochet outside to play, to run, and to be a nine-year-old boy!

The day he chased after my car

Ricochet was in a new school and in his second year of fourth grade. We thought the better school district, and the fact that he'd already mastered this curriculum once, would give him a more relaxed school year. The first few months it actually seemed so.

I found out the hard way how much anxiety Ricochet still had at school one morning that December. I pulled up to the curb in the drop-off line in front of the elementary school's main entrance. Ricochet got out as he had every morning that school year. A safety patrol student then closed the car door. When the car in front of me began moving forward, I followed to exit the parking lot.

I advanced three or four car lengths when I heard a child screaming in utter horror. I looked in my rearview mirror to see Ricochet running right between the moving cars and chasing after me in a total panic. I pulled to the side and stopped the car. I rolled down the window and asked Ricochet if he left his backpack or lunchbox in the car — the only reason I could think of that he'd chase my car through the parking lot, freaking out like that.

He was crying and purely desperate.

"No," he sobbed.

"Why are you crying? Why did you chase my car? You can't run into traffic like that *ever*. You scared me, and you scared the teachers outside that are there to be sure you get inside safely."

"I need you, Momma. Don't leave me. I want to be with you, Momma. I can't be away from you." He was positively inconsolable.

I was stunned. Not only was I shocked that he was so upset, but I had been scared to death for his safety in those few moments I watched him run in front of moving cars in my rearview mirror. I needed time to calm down.

I told him to jump in the back seat, and I pulled the car into a parking space. I turned off the engine so Ricochet and I could talk through whatever was going on. We talked for over an hour right there in our car. I exited the vehicle several times during that period, trying to get him out of the car and into school. It wasn't going to happen. I made a deal with him that he could come back home with me for a couple of hours so he could calm down and settle, but I was bringing him to school at 11 AM, and he would go to class then. He agreed and seemed instantly relieved.

As promised, I brought him back to the school at 11 AM that same day. He seemed willing until we approached the parking lot. Before I even parked the car, he was crying again, begging me to take him back home. *What the heck is going on?* I spent forty-five minutes trying to get him into the school building that time. I got him as far as the threshold of the front door by moving a little at a time, but by then he was screaming and crying and approaching a full-blown meltdown. I probably could have enlisted some help and got him to his classroom, but at what cost? The last thing a ten-year-old boy needs socially is to be physically placed in the classroom while screaming and crying. I decided to take him home for the day. He obviously wasn't fit for school that day anyway.

That was a Friday, and I felt certain this odd behavior would be behind us by Monday. No such luck. Ricochet demanded I go in with him. I agreed to walk him to his classroom door, but told him I would not be staying. I was in yoga pants and a baseball cap because I hadn't had the chance to shower yet!

When we turned the corner to the hall of his classroom, he started to fall apart again. By the time we reached his classroom door, he was crying and pleading and wouldn't go in. His teacher came into the hall and tried to help. We asked him what was upsetting him so we could help him. He couldn't tell us. I was stumped, and his teacher was baffled too, but I was not going to take him home again. He'd have this issue every day if he found that it worked. He had to stay at school this time.

Ricochet and I had been in the hall outside his classroom for about thirty minutes when his Special Education teacher approached her classroom across the hall. She saw that he was struggling and came over. It took a good bit of time and coaxing, but we got him into her classroom, as long as I agreed to stay. His Special Education teacher tried everything to calm him down, even offering him licorice to chew on, but he was spiraling, and we couldn't redirect him.

Ricochet had created quite a connection with the guidance counselor at his new school, Mr. W. Let's call him Mr. Wonderful because he was truly the most wonderful addition to Ricochet's life that school year. Mr. Wonderful was Ricochet's confidant and support when he was having trouble at school, and was available whenever Ricochet needed him.

Ricochet's Special Education teacher radioed down to Mr. Wonderful, and requested that he come to her classroom. He came right away and also attempted to redirect Ricochet's attention. After quite a while, at least thirty minutes more, Mr. Wonderful was finally able to strike a deal with Ricochet. He would have Ricochet come to his office and hang out with him and be his helper as long as Ricochet needed. I walked with them as far as the front door, and then told him goodbye. I held my breath as I exited the building, sure Ricochet would run after me crying again. But he didn't. Mr. Wonderful to the rescue!

The next several mornings, Ricochet had me walk to his classroom with him. He went in on his own and had good days, though. He asked to see Mr. Wonderful every day for a couple of weeks to help him feel more secure at school as well. After that, they were out of school for two weeks for the holidays, and then it seemed Ricochet was back to his (special) normal. He jumped out at the curb and went into school as he had done before this odd episode. We never figured out what had triggered it.

I, on the other hand, didn't go back to "normal" so quickly. I had PTSD (Post-Traumatic Stress Disorder) from watching him run into traffic chasing my car that day. Every single time I dropped him off at the curb after that, the remaining 150+ days of the school year, I kept my car still and watched him until I knew he wasn't going to turn back toward the car. My heart pounded, my hands would sweat, my mind raced as I approached the curb. I was panicked each time I dropped him off. It was a traumatic experience and something I'm still not quite over. A year later, I still hesitate to pull away and watch him intently at drop-off. We worked through it (and survived it) though.

The night we didn't hear the doorbell

Ricochet and his cousin, Creative H, still liked to spend time together. Despite the gender difference, they are close in age and often do well together. On occasion, Creative H would spend the night at our house or Ricochet would stay with her. This particular night, Ricochet was with Creative H at her house, just a couple of miles from our home.

Ricochet had been having frequent problems with fear episodes for a few months. He could get very upset remembering something scary he had seen, and had to be with me right away and for a good amount of time to work through it. He struggled to get that scary thought out of his head, which terrified him. This particular week he had not had one fear episode. I warned Auntie and Uncle M that he had been having some difficulties at night, but that this week had been A-Okay.

Auntie and I kept a text conversation going that night, checking in on Ricochet to be sure he was doing well. Around 8:30 or 9 PM I asked her if Ricochet wanted to call me to say goodnight. He did not. I took that as a sign that all would be well. I went about my evening and fell asleep by 10 o'clock.

I awoke the next morning to find a barrage of missed calls and texts from both Auntie and Uncle M. Ricochet had gotten scared around 11:30 PM and, try as they might, they couldn't make it better. They tried calling me, but I forgot to leave my ringer on that night. I called Auntie right away.

"I see you guys called last night. I'm so, so sorry I didn't hear it. Is everything okay?"

"It's okay. He's fine now. He just got scared last night and wanted to go home," she explained.

My heart sank. I felt like #1 Bad Momma for not being accessible when my family needed me. The guilt was heavy and overwhelming. I offered to come pick him up right then, but she said he was doing well. She didn't want him to think he'd be sent home early as if he was bad after having a rough night at their house. *Thanks, Auntie!*

So I arrived to pick him up a little before 11 AM, the time we originally set. I apologized profusely over and over and over again as Ricochet packed his things and got his shoes on. I felt so awful that I inadvertently put them through that. Auntie and Uncle M both assured me it was okay.

Ricochet and I walked next-door to Grandma and Papaw's house directly after. On the way over, I asked him about being scared during the night and apologized to him, too, for not hearing the phone. I told him if it were really urgent, they would have come to our house and let us know in person.

Ricochet looked up at me, and said, "We did go to our house."

"What, Buddy?" I asked, perplexed.

"Uncle M packed my stuff, and we got in his car and went to our house. He knocked on the door and rang the doorbell, but you and Daddy didn't wake up."

I fought my quivering lip. "You did? I'm so sorry, sweetie. Really sorry! Momma always wants to be available for you when you need me."

Needless to say, I called my sister and apologized some more to her and Uncle M. I sent a text of gratitude to Uncle M as well. They assured me it was okay. They hadn't told me about coming to our house and not getting an answer, because they didn't want me to feel any worse than I already did. But I did — I felt much, much worse. I felt like I put everyone through that unnecessarily.

Uncle M responded to my text later, "Ricochet and I share a common bond both having ADHD. Frustrating, yes, but I understand his struggles. I'm glad he was able to finally get to sleep." My heart melted, and I could no longer control the tears.

We all later agreed that it was probably better for Ricochet that he didn't come home that night anyway. He got to see that he could make it through hard times without Momma.

How do I cope?

Parenting a child with ADHD is so much more emotionally and physically demanding, not to mention entirely unpredictable, and I'll never be able to wrap it up in a neat little package. I'll never have total control over it, no matter how many articles, essays, or books I write that may give an assumption to the contrary. That's the entire nature of ADHD anyhow, *not* having total control.

I'm often asked how I cope with my son's ADHD. There certainly isn't a special formula. I didn't sit down and write up a plan: "How I'm Going to Survive a Child with ADHD." Coping is a one-day-at-a-time skill. It's a one-foot-in-front-of-the-other sort of thing. I made every effort to take life each day, each hour, each minute. Some minutes I coped well, and some minutes I crumpled under the pressure. The more time that passed since Ricochet's diagnosis, the greater the percentage of my life's minutes were successfully coping with parenting a child with ADHD.

First, to preserve some sanity, I had to stop fretting about every little difference that was a challenge for Ricochet (and for our family) and start celebrating the many wonderful aspects of his being. It was certainly hard to do deep in the trenches of a public meltdown, and that's where actual "coping" came in.

The root of coping lies in perception. Staying positive is paramount. How I stayed positive in the thick of things sometimes, I honestly don't know (and I didn't always). At some point, I said to myself, I can either feel sorry for my son and sorry for myself, or I can work really hard to focus on the wonderful things. If my radar was tuned only to the negative, I'd miss opportunities for joy.

Coping, by definition, means contending with difficulties and acting to overcome them. Our family copes with a meltdown, homework struggles, seemingly constant calls from school, sensory issues, and constant activity and chatter. But we don't cope with ADHD. We accept ADHD and then teach ourselves to look beyond it. I look right past it as if I don't see it and delight in the wonderful gifts of my special child instead.

Honestly, coping is a game of strategy I play with myself.

First, I *chose* not to wallow. This wild monster, this neurological difference, this ADHD, is part of Ricochet for good. It can't be fixed or cast off. It's part of who he is, and it's part of our family. I could mope, cry, and wish it away and always feel bad because that won't change anything. Or, I could take a stand against ADHD and use my energy to affect change, knowing my son and I would feel better by taking action.

I had to remember to pick my battles and not sweat the small stuff. Ricochet humming while doing his math worksheet may be annoying, but it isn't a big deal — let him hum. Walking into the street to cross without first looking both ways for oncoming traffic, however, is a very big deal and must be tackled. If I tried to change every little negative characteristic of ADHD that manifests in Ricochet, I would go crazy and I wouldn't succeed. I try to accept the small stuff, but battle when safety is at stake. This gave me more minutes of calm most days.

By all means, I had to secure and maintain a healthy sense of humor, too. Some ADHD behaviors are aggravating, frustrating, or embarrassing only when I allow them to be. Ricochet often puts his arms up in the air and swiftly opens them out wide when we approach automatic doors to enter a retail establishment, as though he's using THE FORCE to open the doors. I could certainly be embarrassed by that. People around us often look at him as though he's weird when he does this. But I think it's cute and funny, and it's Ricochet — it's part of his *Star Wars*-loving being. I have accepted it. What's the big deal?

And that's it precisely! I have to consistently say to myself, "What's the big deal?" Then I know I'm coping. I strive to laugh about, accept, and move beyond the small stuff. I find humor in his quirks, for laughter is great medicine.

Most important to coping though, is having faith that all will be okay. I believe my child is going to be happy and successful in the long run. I don't hope for it, now I believe it. I work to nurture his talents, gifts, and passions and guide him to a bright future.

I'm not that kind of mom

I wasn't born to be a mom.

Wait. That didn't come out right. What I mean is, I wasn't born to be *just* a mom. Well, that didn't come out right, either. I don't think being "only" a mom is a bad thing. In fact, I envy those "I'm-a-mom-with-my-whole-being" type of women. I am not that kind of mom.

I'm far from perfect. Far, far from a storybook "perfect" mom. A mom who spends all her children's waking hours interacting with them: baking magazine-worthy goodies; joining their game of tag; decorating for every holiday like Martha Stewart.

I suffered monumental guilt for not being that kind of mom. I love my kids, and I want them to have the very best lives possible. The problem is, if I want them to have perfect lives, then I must make it happen: make them eat fruits and vegetables; keep the house neat and germ-free; I should head a committee or two for the PTA; and volunteer at the soup kitchen. That's how you create great kids, right? Kids who grow up to be happy, successful, fulfilled adults.

Yes.

No.

Oh hell, who knows?

If this fantasy "happy" family is your family, I'm in awe of you. My family will never be that perfect, and trying to make it so would likely make us all anything but happy.

Striving for perfection causes anxiety, fear, and low self-esteem. No one is perfect. No one.

Believe me, I know. If you don't believe me, ask my family.

You see, for me to create a picture-perfect family would be a farce. It wouldn't be authentic. It would be crafted from a desire to be something I'm not. I've struggled for years feeling like an inadequate mom because my kids demand mostly foods that are shrink-wrapped, my house is a disaster I can't let anyone outside our immediate circle see, and I have never once been to a meeting of the PTA, not one. My time has been consumed caring in a different way. I strain to change these things, and I traumatize my family. Aiming to be the "perfect mom" just makes life worse instead of better in this house.

Instead, I'm the mom who spends hours researching ADHD, learning disabilities, anxiety, organization strategies, etc. I'm the one who goes to school conferences and IEP meetings and emails teachers multiple times a week. I'm the mom that drives across town to therapy visits and routine doctor appointments. I'm the mom who takes her girl out for cake and hot cocoa to be sure she knows she's loved. I'm the mom who reciprocates hugs every single chance she gets, and then some. I'm the mom who is here, day in and day out, for whatever my children need. I may not be in the kitchen with them making cupcakes or on the floor mock-crashing Hot Wheels cars every day, but I am spending just as much time trying to ensure their success and happiness, in my own way.

Recognizing this has actually given me some peace.

So I'll go on feeling good that my kids had a shower and three pseudo-meals today. We'll continue to celebrate clearing life's hurdles with dinner at a restaurant instead of a fancy home-cooked meal with a blue-ribbon-worthy all-American pie a-la-mode. And I'll continue to fight for the success of my children in the not-so-perfect way I know how.

I finally accepted that I'm not that kind of mom, and I'm okay with that.

Glimpses of hope

My special child, this bright and creative child with ADHD, can be such a challenge to parent. I've watched him bounce around in our neurotypical world, stumbling and falling more than his peers. I've wanted to fix it and make it all better from day one, as though ADHD is just a boo-boo.

It's not.

I can't.

At some point in this special parenting journey, I came to accept that ADHD couldn't be changed. I even came to accept ADHD into our lives, as part of our family, and redirected my focus on the great abilities Ricochet has in spite of ADHD.

I focus on my children's talents and accomplishments and love them unconditionally. Sure, I'm going to worry about Ricochet's future a bit more than Warrior Girl's; I am human. But the time will come when he is no longer under the safe harbor of my wing. I must concentrate on his abilities and teach him to soar on his own. I need to do that for both my children, but it will take more effort for Ricochet.

Ricochet often lends me glimpses of his future, illustrating that he's going to be okay. Not just okay, but great, even. Quite often, these glimpses are hidden in the briefest moments of peace and joy — often times when I am in his company and realize I'm not worried for him. When he creates something unique, says something insightful, or achieves something not so easy for his peers, I focus on his abilities and how they'll serve him well in adulthood, and I feel satisfied. It's often in these little, always fleeting moments that I realize I'm at peace with ADHD.

I've seen glimpses of Ricochet's future potential the day he fished for three hours without even a nibble on his line; the day he cheered me on to climb the lighthouse stairs behind him; the day a snowball fight with his Papaw turned into a thoughtful and strategic combat; the time we had to camp out in our own home when we were snowed in; the time he took living with his grandparents for two months in stride. All of these things were unexpected in light of his ADHD and brought me great faith in his outlook. I could finally let myself believe in his fulfilling future.

Keep looking out the windshield

I felt hopeless many times over the first few years after Ricochet's diagnosis. It was tough to parent a child with ADHD, especially without concrete instructions. Each time I considered how I'd lost hope from time to time, I was reminded of a talk I attended by a very wise real estate coach and motivational speaker. His program is a system to build business where the broker will inevitably hear "no" many, many times every day. He is very motivational so brokers don't slip into the trap of feeling personally rejected. He spoke about keeping a positive attitude the last time I saw him, and said something that resonated with me in relation to my life with a child with ADHD.

"You must look out the windshield," he proclaimed with great conviction. "If you're looking down [in sadness or defeat], how can you see where you're going? If you're looking back in your rearview mirror, you are sure to crash then as well. Keep looking out the windshield. Keep your eyes on the horizon in front of you," he said enthusiastically. "This will provide the best chance of effectively moving forward toward your goals. You must always look forward."

It took nearly four years to learn to effectively parent my child with ADHD. Four years of roller-coaster peaks and valleys and frequent trial by fire. But through the challenges I discovered my strength, courage, resilience, determination, and simple gratitude for the small stuff.

I made it through, and I'm here to tell you, it's so much better on the downhill slope of this treacherous learning curve. There are still ups and downs — but now I know how to handle the curveballs, for the most part. I understand my son and his needs now, even the fact that what he needs isn't always his momma hovering close by to swoop in and fix things.

I have forward momentum now and I will keep looking out the windshield. I will take what I've learned on this journey and use it as the fuel to propel us forward further, all the while looking out the windshield, my eyes on the beautiful horizon in front of me.

Thank you for reading!

Dear Reader,

I hope you enjoyed *Boy Without Instructions: Surviving the Learning Curve of Parenting a Child with ADHD*. Writing this book has been both cathartic and rewarding. I imagine you are wondering how Ricochet is doing now and what his future holds. For updates on my special boy for many years to come, follow my blog at BoyWithoutInstructions.com, and Facebook.com/PennyWilliamsAuthor. Will he grow up to be a happy and successful adult? I sure hope so!

When I managed my former blog, {a mom's view of ADHD}, I received numerous emails from readers thanking me for sharing our journey and compiling ADHD resources. As an author, I love feedback, so that was very rewarding. You and your family are the reason I will continue to write about ADHD. So, tell me what you liked, what you loved, and even what you hated about this book. I would truly love to hear from you. Write to me at penny@pennywilliamsauthor.com and visit me online at PennyWilliamsAuthor.com.

I need to ask a favor. I'd love a review of *Boy Without Instructions*. Positive or negative, I need your feedback. Reviews are tough to come by, but they can make or break the success of a book and its author. If you can spare just five minutes, please visit the *Boy Without Instructions* pages on Amazon.com and Goodreads.com and submit your candid review.

Thank you for reading *Boy Without Instructions* and riding along on my journey with Ricochet. Look for my next book, *What to Expect When You're NOT Expecting ADHD* in late 2014 or early 2015.

With sincerest gratitude,
Penny Williams

Get more guidance and mentoring with Penny Williams, a.k.a., the ADHD Momma!

What to Expect When Parenting Children with ADHD

The Insider's Guide to ADHD

The contrast between expectations and genuine capability is stark but invisible with ADHD, creating challenges every moment in all aspects of life. Use *What to Expect* and the 25+ worksheets included to learn about your child's behaviors, triggers, strengths, and weaknesses, to improve life for your child with ADHD, and your entire family.

The Insider's Guide to ADHD bypasses the reward charts, strict limits, and other standard recommendations to get to the root of the true formula for effective ADHD parenting. Inside, you'll find twelve positive parenting strategies for ADHD that all lead to one universal truth for creating success in the lives of kids with ADHD, and their families.

Purchase Penny's other titles on Amazon.com, BarnesandNoble.com, and through other select retailers.

ONLINE COURSES

Penny's online school, the **Parenting ADHD & Autism Academy**, offers online training for challenged parents. The courses guide and mentor parents raising kids with ADHD and/or high-functioning autism. Penny teaches you where to start when diagnosed, parenting strategies specific to ADHD and autism, behavior modification, how to work with schools, parent self-care, setting your child up for success, and much more. Visit the academy at **ParentingADHDandAutismAcademy. com** to learn more and register for courses.

WEBSITE

Visit **ParentingADHDandAutism.com** for effective tips and strategies in several formats: articles, sharing quality resources, how-to videos, online courses, and parent coaching.

Endnotes

[1] McLeod, S. A., "Type A Personality." Simply Psychology. N.p., n.d. Web 26 Mar. 2014. <http://www.simplypsychology.org/personality-a.html>

[2] Hartle, T.M., "Pitocin induced labor doubles the risk of ADHD." NaturalNews. N.p., n.d. Web 26 Mar. 2014. <http://www.naturalnews.com/033259_pitocin_ADHD.html>

[3] Smith, Melinda, and Robert Segal, "ADD / ADHD in Children: Signs and Symptoms of Attention Deficit Disorder." HelpGuide. N.p., n.d. Web. 25 Mar. 2014. <http://www.helpguide.org/mental/adhd_add_signs_symptoms.htm>

[4] Lim, Jeanette, "OCR Memorandum: Schools Must Evaluate Children Who May Have Attention Deficit Disorders (ADD)." WrightsLaw. N.p., 1 Jan. 2000. Web, 26 Mar. 2014. <http://www.wrightslaw.com/info/add.eval.ocrmemo.htm>

[5] Zeigler Dendy, Chris. "The ABCs of ADD and ADHD." Teens with ADHD. N.p., n.d. Web. 25 Mar. 2014. <http://chrisdendy.com/abc.htm>

[6] "Nebo Autism." Nebo Autism. N.p., n.d. Web. 26 Mar. 2014. <http://neboautism.wordpress.com/page/3/>

[7] "helicopter parent." Dictionary.com. Dictionary.com Unabridged. Random House, Inc. N.p., n.d. Web. 8 Feb. 2014. <http://dictionary.reference.com/browse/helicopter parent>

Made in the USA
Coppell, TX
04 June 2021

56900257R00177